T0149192

Ms. Thang
Goes Back to School
Survival Lessons from a Substitute Teacher

BARBARA MILES

authorHOUSE®

AuthorHouse™
1663 Liberty Drive
Bloomington, IN 47403
www.authorhouse.com
Phone: 1 (800) 839-8640

Published by AuthorHouse   11/18/2015

ISBN: 978-1-5049-5272-9 (sc)
ISBN: 978-1-5049-5273-6 (e)

Library of Congress Control Number: 2015916774

Print information available on the last page.

This book is printed on acid-free paper.

Dedication

To classroom teachers at all levels of our education system, I share your joy and feel your pain. Specifically to the teachers at Middle Town (pardon the pseudonym), although I made a quick retreat, please know that I will never forget your kindness.

Acknowledgments

A big shout out to my family and friends who volunteered such big support for my little book. Hope everyone has as much fun reading as we did developing it. But as we all realized, our goal of capturing the attention of a broad audience to focus on some of the dysfunctions in our school systems is a much larger challenge. As mothers, fathers, aunts, uncles and grandparents, we all share very personal and vested interests in the success of our schools.

Special thanks to my niece and author, Katrina Covington Whitmore, who was first to encourage me to take my journal off the shelf and finish the book. (Check out Katrina's four books: *The Bride of the Desert Trilogy* and *Say Yes*.) Then there's my friend and volunteer reviewer, Lindley Cole, whose edits and comments were spot on. Thank you so much for your time and sincere interest. As always, my loving niece Coni Howard and sisters Ruby Moman and Velma Covington lent eager eyes and ears for measuring each step of the project's development. And, yes Ted, your feedback was helpful too.

Let's not forget my Atlanta family, the Reddings, who paved the path and orchestrated a smooth transition when I decided to relocate to Atlanta. Kim, Eric, Erika, Ralph, Jean, Marcel, I will always appreciate your warm embrace and thoughtful guidance as I navigated my way through the big ATL.

To my daughter, BFF and enduring creative energy partner, Denise Pruitt, your work is just beginning as we continue the conversation on the web site, **TeachersTalkNow.com.** I am blessed to have you at the helm of my talented team of communication specialists. And, while they may not know it, we are drafting your brother, Kevin, and his social media savvy children, Kara, Kelsey and Justin, into service to bring their skills and talents to the project going forward. Also, I salute "my other daughter," Catherine Irish, for the exemplary job you do everyday monitoring my grands' educational progress, equipping them with the knowledge and skills that their future successes will demand. As our former first lady so astutely observed, it does indeed take a village.

Finally, kudos to Rosalyn Strain who generously contributed time and talent designing a set of artfully crafted collages with faces and places from the Chocolate Singles Magazine years. Thank you one and all.

Preface

When I signed on for a substitute teacher position some years ago, I skipped to my new job bubbling with enthusiasm. I had emerged from a crowded field of applicants and was thrilled at the prospect of returning to my first calling, teaching, at the start of my professional career. Now a grandmother, the thought of again molding young minds and hearts with an appetite for learning was just the incentive I needed to get up and out again after an extended hiatus from the world of work and life in general.

Some of you may remember "Ms. Thang," a.k.a. Barbara Miles, the publisher and editor of Chocolate Singles Magazine, a widely acclaimed, nationally distributed publication based in New York City that made its pioneering debut on the burgeoning singles stage in the early 1980s. Cited by such venerated oracles as The New York Times and the Wall Street Journal for setting the advertising world on fire with the emergence of a new niche market, CS revolutionized the path to love and marriage for this new demographic. It was the first publication to introduce classified personal ads to an audience of middle income Black American singles…."Buppies."

Suddenly, closet introvert that I am, I was catapulted onto the stage of national television talk shows, with frequent appearances on the likes of the Phil Donahue Show, Oprah's predecessor. Being dubbed the principal media spokesperson for the emerging Black singles market, I was seen so frequently on some local TV shows that many thought I was on the programs' payroll.

Chocolate Singles soon expanded its turf to include a travel and leisure club that introduced its subscribers to star-studded, record-setting singles only parties at such popular New York venues as the Palladium, Studio 54, the Red Parrot, Copacabana, Underground and the U.S.S. Intrepid. CS members cruised the Caribbean, skied the

Poconos and traveled to the islands of St. Lucia, Jamaica, Barbados, St. Thomas, the Bahamas and other exotic destinations that were formerly just names in somebody else's travelogue. The line-up of celebrities frequenting CS events included Eddie Murphy, The Jacksons, Mike Tyson at the height of his fame, NFL Hall of Famer Lawrence Taylor and other sports heroes too numerous to name. One ecstatic local journalist summed up the fun at a Chocolate Singles event declaring, "I thought I'd died and gone to heaven!"

When Chocolate Singles ceased operations after a fifteen-year run, I readily surrendered the limelight, packed up bags and baggage and fled to Atlanta for a long overdue respite. But, unaccustomed as I was to a life of leisure, it wasn't long before the doldrums set in. Battling an acute case of cabin fever, a new ailment for which I lacked coping mechanisms, I felt the need to return to work.

Apparently, this was a view shared by one of my new Atlanta friends. As I lounged around with too much time on my hands, I was scolded for my idleness. "Everybody I know is still working," she informed me rather brusquely.

A return to teaching was a natural selection since it was a field in which I had previously experienced a substantial amount of success. Thus, substitute teaching would be my introduction to the local school system while I sorted out the particulars of re-entry into a full-time work schedule.

But it wasn't long after I set foot in my first classroom assignment that I discovered a different world than the one I had known before. Schools, it seems, have migrated in some strange and often baffling ways into the 21st century. As I tackled my new job, I began to experience first-hand the enormity of challenges teachers now face on a daily basis. Spoiler alert: I lasted all of three long weeks before getting my come-uppance and bouncing back to the future of today's schools. As one of my more belligerent students put it, "Ms. Miles may look like a diva, but she's old." Yeah! Slam! That hit a nerve. But let me not get ahead of the story.

Everything I read and hear in today's media leads me to believe that things have not changed a whole lot since my brief subbing sojourn. In fact, as my teacher friends assert and news headlines confirm, they have, if anything, gotten worse. Why politicians and some government officials find it profitable to declare war on teachers is, in my opinion, beyond baffling. Who, with good intentions, would think it advantageous to attack the people with whom we entrust our children for education the better part of their waking hours?

I'm reminded of how back in the day one of the jokes often repeated by the husband of one of my colleagues was this: "My wife doesn't work: She teaches school." Ha! Unfortunately, it seems that many of today's critics still hold that opinion. I would invite those launching concerted attacks on teachers to get up off your insular perches and take a quick walk with me on the wild side of today's classrooms to acquaint yourselves with the difficulties and complexities of the job before brandishing your weapons.

Okay. So I have to get on my soap-box and say that nowadays teachers, whose work doesn't end when the closing bell rings, are virtually without a voice or public advocates to counteract the sometimes vicious and often sustained assaults from their critics. Unions have been decimated, budgets slashed, schools closed, classrooms overcrowded and even access to some very basic supplies limited. Yet, accountability for the failure of our schools to attain unrealistic goals seems to rest squarely and unfairly on their shoulders.

Most teachers, in my educated opinion, are unsung heroes. They are, for the most part, guardians of a sacred trust, aspiring to educate our children—beyond basic skills needed to pass tests—with knowledge essentials for productive performance in an ever changing world. Yet, they are among the lowest paid and least respected professionals in our society. After reading some recent "bad teacher" headlines, I was persuaded to share my story; that of an outsider's inside view of life in today's schools from the vantage point of the beleaguered teacher.

You can't know, unless you've experienced it just what the job of teaching is like. I salute those women and men who enter their classrooms every day hardly expecting to be greeted with an apple on their desk. I especially salute the teachers at "Middle Town" Elementary School in the exurban Georgia community where I substituted. To those teachers: If you read this, you'll know who you are and the real name of your school. You were among the best and, despite the lack of support from a detached and often hostile administration, could cite innumerable success stories. Please know that there are those among us who greatly appreciate the work you do and the personal sacrifices you make to achieve that success. And for prospective substitutes rushing with wide-eyed wonder to your new teaching assignments, let me prepare you for some of the surprises that may await you in this 21st century wonderland.

I suspect that virtually every classroom teacher has a story to tell. If any of you are so inclined, I invite you to share your stories about the good, the bad and the ugly aspects of teaching with us at **TeachersTalkNow.com.**

Chapter One

—⟋⟍⟍—

The Community Classroom

The three-hour orientation session was held in a fifth grade elementary school classroom. Really. We, the chosen ones, crouched meekly in our seats like good little students fully engaged in our lesson, or doing a damn good job of faking it.

"Are there any questions?" the instructor asked, while rapidly packing her gear, signaling the end of the lecture as she prepared to bolt for the exit.

Silence. We sat obediently on our hands. Not a creature was stirring.

What circumstances had brought this unlikely gathering of dissimilar souls to this classroom, I wondered. I stole a glance at the recently retired teacher whose fixed income was perhaps coming up a bit short to sustain her lifestyle in today's economy. Then I eyed the teacher wannabes; some of whom were under-qualified for full-time positions and others, interns majoring in education seeking to jump-start their careers. Several transferees from other school systems had also answered Wilton County's cast call for substitute teachers while waiting for permanent openings consistent with their credentials and experience.

Questions? No, there were no questions. We had made the cut; what else was there to know.

But did my non-traditional classmates know what they were getting into? Probably not. I suspect the unemployed former TV journalist may have imagined she was signing on to become a guest lecturer. The out-of-work financial analyst whose office had been downsized in a company merger may have thought he could just make regular classroom appearances as role model for the day. And surely the computer programmer and other tech sector geeks whose jobs had been outsourced to India were confident that they could lure children of all ages into their temples of knowledge with their deft command of icons and iPads. Even I, a former teacher and erstwhile magazine publisher, didn't delay the instructor's departure with my usual probing questions.

In better economic times, many of us would have been actively courted by eager headhunters looking to pocket a fat fee by auctioning us off to the highest corporate bidders. But that was then and this was now. Jobs of any kind are hard enough to come by, and I, like my classmates, needed to go back to work.

Once I made up my mind to take the plunge, I applied to several school districts in my area for a substitute teacher position. Imagine my surprise when prospective employers weren't particularly impressed with my resume! When I called back to check my status in one district, the human resource administrator informed me rather tersely that I just had to be patient. "You need to understand," she stated haughtily, "we routinely get considerably more applications than we have openings, and you will just have to wait your turn."

For me, it was a rather rude awakening. Until then, never in my long and varied career had I ever imagined that I would have to stand in line for a substitute teaching job. Obviously, "over-qualified" is a term that has been erased from the vocabulary of today's HR snobs.

But it seems that job opportunities, as with most things in life, are a matter of feast or famine because, wouldn't you know it, two offers came simultaneously from neighboring school districts, Wilton and Marshview. I opted for Wilton simply because the hourly pay scale was a few dollars higher, a consideration at which I wasn't inclined to scoff.

Some school districts have an observation requirement for new subs, which is essentially a one-day commitment to sit in on one or more classes during regular school hours. Wilton County had no such requirement, but I thought it was a good idea. So I created a bit of a stir coming out of the starting gate with my "observation" request.

Schools can be very regimented institutions. In general, they don't take kindly to departures from normal procedures. There was no paragraph, not even a footnote, in this particular district's rulebook about observation opportunities for prospective substitutes. But to their credit, Wilton rose to the occasion and endeavored to accommodate me. Thus, my reintroduction to the world of education since my long-ago days of teaching was at a well-organized, high-achieving middle school.

After my daylong visit, I was inspired. What I didn't realize was that I had apparently been paired with the most gifted teacher in one of the best schools in the county.

When I entered Mrs. Long's classroom, escorted by one of the assistant principals, she hardly looked up to acknowledge our presence. I tried to remain inconspicuous, taking a seat in the back of the room as the AP quietly made her exit. The teacher was obviously in the middle of a lesson and endeavored to ignore the interruption. I surmised that visitors were often steered her way.

The look of Mrs. Long's classroom, first and foremost, told the story: a lot of learning was going on here. I was dazzled. The first thing that caught my attention was a display of dioramas depicting various stages in the evolution of man. Compositions mounted on bulletin boards around the room attested to the fact that the students who constructed these visuals were thoroughly familiar with the history they portrayed. Collages told another aspect of the story— early man's interaction with his environment. And an attractive, neatly organized interest center, replete with a sofa and two huge fluffy floor cushions (Can you believe it!) offered an appealing array of books, computers—all Internet connected—magazines, video and audio tapes for small group and independent study.

This teacher was a joy to behold. She never raised her voice (only her eyebrows) but occasionally tapped softly on her desk to get the students' attention. Participation in class discussions was animated. These eager minds just couldn't wait to be expanded. When they took a test, all of them appeared to be fully engaged. The ones who finished early tiptoed over to the teacher to have their work checked, after which they busied themselves with some special project from the abundant options in the interest center.

I was sold! This was important work. Minds were being molded, horizons expanded. This was the face of the future. I could sink my teeth into this.

The list of 40 things every substitute teacher should know distributed by the orientation class instructor included the following nuggets: a general admonishment to always be positive and avoid negativism (no further instructions on this point); tips on avoiding gossip and rumors; advice on how to acquaint oneself with the curriculum (a neat trick when the substitute is called the evening before or the morning of the assignment); cautions against becoming too familiar with the students; and this one, which ultimately was of particular concern to me: *Don't deal directly with parents. Parents should never come to the classroom without a pass from the office.*

While recognizing that the stuff presented to us was pretty superficial, I had sat serenely through my three-hours. After all, what was there really to be apprehensive about? I wasn't a novice. I was a veteran of two big city school systems where I had been a certified, highly rated teacher, and ultimately promoted out of the classroom to become a college administrator at a well-respected New York City campus. So I knew education from the ground up. Hell, I could teach anybody's class and probably the teachers too, if truth were told. Or so I thought.

Who am I?

Good question. Back in my publishing heyday, friends dubbed me "Ms. Thang." Okay. Translate successful entrepreneur and accomplished wordsmith who knows how to strut her stuff. If they only knew the truly reticent, compulsive workaholic who hides behind that façade! Give me one job and I'll find a way to elevate it to two, sweating bullets all the way. Maybe that's because I've been working practically my whole life; got my first job at fourteen years old. I've always set pretty high performance standards for myself, which I too often take to bed with me at the expense of a good night's sleep.

In the early 80's, enticed by the lure of entrepreneurship, I decided to try my hand at publishing. As it developed, I hit the right market niche at the right time because my small, independent, low-budget magazine took off at warp speed, becoming an instant success. Some of you may have read about Chocolate Singles in the New York Times, N. Y. Daily News, Wall Street Journal, Essence Magazine and other major publications. Many of my subscribers saw my face so frequently on The Phil Donahue Show (Remember him? Ruled daytime talk before Oprah) and local TV channels that they thought I was on the programs' payroll. To media far and near, I became the "it" girl; face of the first singles magazine to target my underserved demographic. And, if you lived in New York, who could forget those star-studded, singles-only parties that jam-packed such popular venues as the Palladium, Studio 54, The Red Parrot, Copacabana and The Underground.

Chocolate Singles Magazine had a good run for nearly fifteen years, but eventually the declining market for print publications took its toll. Although my audience was increasing, advertising dollars had become so fiercely competitive that even such industry titans as Time Warner and Conde Nast were taking a serious walloping. My small company couldn't tread water forever, so after the simultaneous dissolution of my magazine and third bad marriage, I fled to Atlanta for a long overdue hiatus from love and life in general.

Happy Dayz
Chocolate Singles Sampler – Faces & Places

More CS Friends & Faces

After two years of idleness, interspersed by a sprinkling of volunteer work here and there, I found myself suffering from a malady I had never experienced in my entire life—an acute case of cabin fever. It seemed everybody I knew was working but me. It was like I could find my way to the mall blindfolded and my car would steer itself automatically to my favorite parking space. I became so predictable that one of my friends once came looking for me at the mall when I failed to answer my cell phone, located my car in its usual parking spot and came directly to my favorite store to ferret me out.

When I wasn't bargain chasing, I found myself sinking into daylong doldrums filled with an endless cycle of cable news networks and crossword puzzles. I was reminded of the wife whose husband complained about his difficulty adjusting to her early retirement when her normal lively and informed dinner table conversation had digressed to daily updates on the latest soap opera trysts. I, too, was becoming irrelevant. There is nothing like extended idleness to breed a better understanding of a good old-fashioned work ethic.

A return to teaching would be more than a means of making strained financial ends meet. I wasn't down to my last dime and, with a few lifestyle adjustments, could survive. But I *wanted* to go back to work. Going back to my original calling represented an opportunity to become relevant again, to make a contribution to the collective value system of the next generation. I felt abundantly motivated. I was going to help save the world—one child at a time.

Panic was about to overtake me when, after satisfying all the eligibility requirements, including background checks and finger printing, I sat around several days waiting for the phone to ring. Then the call came. It was for an elementary school located in a somewhat remote eastern Atlanta suburb that was about a 45-minute drive from my home.

Friends couldn't understand why I would be interested in an assignment that involved so much travel, but I wasn't worried. I was a seasoned business traveler. In New York, the trip to my office in the Borough of Queens from the great white elephant of a suburban estate that had been my ex-husband's ultimate fantasy was an hour at best by car. In traffic, which was always unpredictable, it could easily be stretched by another half hour or more. So I was well conditioned for this little trek. As long as I didn't get lost, I would get there with time to spare.

My first assignment was a fifth grade class in an ethnically integrated, predominantly Caucasian community that was actually more exurban than suburban. In some respects, it reminded me of my old New York neighborhood that was located on the outer fringes of an advancing urban sprawl where the mini mansions of the community's new social elites lived side-by-side with the modest country cottages of third and fourth generation inhabitants. This was that, minus the mini mansions.

The school was a new construction in its first year of operation. Its lackluster architecture wasn't a likely candidate for any awards; except for the abundant windows, it was easily mistaken for a one-story industrial plant. As I crossed the threshold of my new career, I sniffed the lingering scent of plaster and paint that new buildings seem reluctant to surrender.

I had started out in the dark, anxious to get there and get situated before the children arrived. The sun was just peeking over the horizon as I walked through the school's nondescript entrance.

In retrospect, I was Alice in Wonderland falling obliviously into a deep, dark and uncertain rabbit hole. Like Alice, I was equally unsuspecting of the abundant array of surprises my substituting future would hold.

Now, having emerged on the other side, I am writing this survival manual for others like me, new recruits who rush with wide-eyed wonder toward the uncertainties of their new substitute teaching assignments. Perhaps I can alert you to a few of the pitfalls in your brave new world before you take a similar plunge.

Chapter Two

Rules of Engagement

Rule 1: Do a reality check.

In wonderland, things are rarely what they seem. I was soon to gain a better appreciation of the old adage: If it sounds too good to be true, it's probably just that.

My first day of subbing was entirely manageable and unbelievably exhilarating. The absent fifth grade teacher, Mrs. Kane, had left model lesson plans. Besides the basics, which accounted for nearly every minute of the school day, there were numerous helpful notations. A schedule for daily specials (art, music and physical education) was neatly charted; library privileges were explained, as were interest center activities; line leaders had been designated to avoid a mad scramble for the coveted positions; and names taped to the students' desks facilitated identification, a critical asset on that first day when the substitute is attempting to establish rapport. There was even a well-defined point system for rewarding good behavior.

I ended my first day feeling entirely successful, but the plan was so well written and the students so disciplined that a robot could probably have executed it. Still, I felt empowered when other teachers in the fifth grade cluster noted that they hadn't heard a peep out of the class all day. It was true; the students had been exceptionally well behaved and motivated.

In all honesty, I have to concede that the magic was not of my making, and the fact that these children had such good work habits was no accident of fate. I would guess that they had the potential to be as disorderly as any other class. But it was immediately apparent that a system of controls was in place. From the moment they entered the classroom, they knew what was expected of them throughout the day.

A soft buzz had permeated the room as students greeted each other, exchanged pleasantries and speculated about the stranger standing at the door. Substitutes are a familiar sight, so they didn't seem particularly surprised to see me. The bolder ones approached me to ask if their teacher was out for the day, while the rest of them simply hung up their coats and took their seats. The morning assignments left by their teacher were already on the board and they knew what to do. My name was also on the board, but I introduced myself nevertheless.

These fifth graders were challenged throughout the day to perform academically, with numerous opportunities for creative expression. Threats were not necessary. In this environment, the carrot worked better than the stick, and the most effective carrot was spurring them on to feelings of accomplishment.

We quickly established a mutual commitment to our respective goals; they recognized that I was serious about carrying out their teacher's plan, and they were willing to help me over any rough spots. Hands flailed the air vigorously as they competed to give me guidance in interpreting classroom rules and procedures. All of us shared a common goal: to impress the absent teacher with our performances when she returned.

At the end of the day, I was pleased to be asked to stay the whole week. "I like this job," I thought triumphantly, as I left the building after my second day of subbing for Mrs. Kane. Naively, I imagined it could always be like that.

Rule 2: Dress for success.

Enter any public school building in this day and age and the entire staff—from teachers to custodians and everybody in between—is likely to look like they're dressed for a camping trip. In fact, in terms of their dress, teachers these days are often barely distinguishable from the maintenance crew. Many looked like they'd interrupted their gardening to come start the school day.

That's not necessarily bad. We're all more casual nowadays. But, remember, regular teachers have an advantage: their students know who they are. When students first encounter a foreign presence standing at the door to greet them, they ought to know who *you* are, also.

No one ever mistook me for custodial staff. The children's first question to me was always, "Are you gonna be our teacher today?" However casual or comfortable I got, I still tried to look like a teacher. And I can tell you, from first-hand experience, the children respected that effort.

A dress code has never been a problem for me. Love for duds runs deep in my family's blood. Just ask my granddaughter. Some of my best dressed compliments came from her as a preschool tiny tot when she would demonstrate our shared passion for fashion by flinging my purse over her shoulder and strutting across the room chanting, "Look, look at me. I'm Nana and I am so-o-o in fashion."

I recall being besieged by Kelsey when I returned to New York for her fifth birthday party. "What are you wearing to my party?" the little girl kept asking me. Finally, I'd had enough.

"Why do you keep asking me that," I snapped. "Are you bugging everybody else about what they're wearing?" The rebuke registered on her sad little face as she hung her head and solemnly reiterated her elevated expectations for me. "But you are s-o-o-o in fashion."

Yep. Obviously scrutiny starts at an early age.

I had my fair share of admirers in the second grade, including the young tyke who would creep up behind me and start massaging my shoulders. Then there was the little girl who would break ranks with her line whenever she spied me in the hall and rush over to grab my waist for a hug. But my biggest fan club was in the fifth grade; the group I had expected to be hardest to win over based on my past experience as a full-time teacher. My secret weapon? My wardrobe.

At the impressionable age of 10 or 11, fifth graders tend to be great advocates of style. Sure, they've adjusted to the daily dress down trend—jeans and things—of today's teachers, but the teachers who dress *up* get their immediate attention. As substitutes we need all the assets we can muster. If dressing for success means pulling out your designer duds to cultivate a new fan club, why not?

The girls, especially, were attentive to every detail of my appearance. Chantal, for example, the head honcho of the school's fashion police, wanted to know if I dyed my hair and Veronica, her side kick, asked how often I got my nails done. They were surprisingly savvy about designer names, and it stood me in good stead that I habitually wore some familiar names like Calvin Klein, Donna Karan and Ralph Lauren. Yes, I may have taken a financial tumble but, like the impoverished aristocracy of old, we fallen idols have our pride.

One morning, as I stood at the door decked out in a soft russet-colored leather suit with moderately high-heeled boots of the same color, I momentarily stopped traffic. "She's really sharp today!" Cyndi observed. "Yeah, she's way cool," said Krista. But the ultimate compliment came from little Joel in the third grade class: "Are you a supervisor or something?" As I had anticipated, some of the students took one look at my "cool clothes" and decided I was an okay adult. Even if they're into hip-hop or grunge themselves, I think they truly appreciate it when their authority figures look the part.

Two of my new best friends from the fifth grade class would regularly seek me out at recess for some "girl talk," sharing some of their most intimate secrets, many of which I wasn't really trying to know. Case in point: I was lost in thought, patrolling the improvised playground during recess when Ellie and Lynda came running after me, showering me with hugs and hand squeezings.

Ellie was a pleasant chubby girl with a cute round face. She was easily two or more sizes bigger than the other girls in the class and feature for feature rather unremarkable—fair skin, brown eyes, straight brown limp hair, a slightly oversized nose—but she had the most endearing smile, enhanced by pearly white, perfectly shaped teeth. Lynda, on the other hand was thin as a rail, with wild curly hair, beady piercing eyes and a stooped, almost crouching posture that conjured up images of an animal in the wild stalking its prey.

"I quit my boyfriend," Ellie confided, with an approving Lynda at her side.

"Yes," Lynda chimed in without being prodded. "I told her he called her a big fat greasy pig."

"You told her what?" I gasped. This was her best friend?

"Yes," said Lynda unapologetically. "We were on the school bus and his friends were teasing him about Ellie. Then he said, "I don't like that ole big fat pig."

"Oh," I said, moderating my response. I guess this was something Lynda felt Ellie needed to know.

Apparently she thought so too. "I don't like him anymore," Ellie declared nonchalantly. I admired her resilience. Obviously she hadn't been too crushed by boyfriend's rejection.

So what does all of this have to do with the three R's? Everything and nothing. Dressing the part is just one of the tools of the trade for breaking the ice and winning their confidence and ultimately their respect. If they like you, it's a whole lot easier to teach them.

Rule 3: Check your ego at the door

In this business, it helps to be armed with a good self-concept. Know from the outset that you are not your job. If you walk into this arena without a positive self-image, you will soon enough be reduced to a quivering mound of self doubt.

Now remember, I signed on to become a substitute teacher. I don't recall anything in the agreement about a substitute paraprofessional. But when I returned to Middle Town Elementary for my third day of *teaching*, I was in for a big surprise. Nobody had bothered to mention that I would be substituting as a teacher's assistant in a kindergarten classroom.

Okay. I regrouped and decided to roll with it. I had never been anybody's assistant anything in the whole of my professional career. But having traveled 30 miles to the school, it didn't make sense to turn around and go back. So, early bird that I am, I sat in one of the little people's chairs (deeming it not politic to take the only adult chair in the room behind the teacher's desk) and waited for the teacher to arrive.

Mrs. Jennings was a young mother in her first year of teaching. Two big firsts in her life coming together in the same year had left her somewhat befuddled. Overweight and disproportionately round in the middle, perhaps a leftover from her recent pregnancy, she gave the appearance of being someone who waged the perpetual battle of the bulge. The absence of makeup and her nondescript catalog variety apparel suggested that she spent few if any of her mornings in the mirror. I would guess that getting the baby settled and getting to work on time was about as much as she could handle.

She seemed surprised and momentarily puzzled to find me waiting in her classroom. I quickly introduced myself: "I'm Barbara Miles, a substitute teacher assigned to assist you today," I said cheerfully.

"Oh, uh, okay," she stammered. Her face registered discomfort. "They didn't tell me they were, uh, sending someone," she said hesitantly. Attempting to collect herself, she asked, "You're uh, Miss...?"

"Barbara Miles. Call me Barbara," I volunteered, attempting to put her at ease. Although she was apparently younger than either of my children, she didn't return the favor. In fact, she never introduced herself by name.

At first there was nothing to do.

"I really don't know what to... uh... what you should be doing," she confessed falteringly. "I mean, I really don't have anything for you to do right now," she added apologetically. I had the impression that she was not used to directing the work of an assistant, particularly one old enough to be her mother. So I began structuring my own role, signaling that I was there to help.

First, I joined her at the door greeting the children as they arrived. Kindergarteners are really adorable, I thought, watching the little people stream through the door, weighed down by backpacks nearly as big as they. Unlike the fifth graders in Mrs. Kane's class, they didn't go directly to their seats. These jittery little five-year-olds seemed to require an inordinate amount of guidance in just about everything they were required to do. Obviously, routines established one day didn't necessarily carry over to the next. Managing this group took a lot of energy. Now, I remembered why I had never wanted to teach below the third grade.

I sat silently observing for the first 45 minutes or so sizing up the cast of characters. It was easy to spot the troublemakers, seated as they were on either side of the teacher's desk. One was a jittery little boy, a tad smaller than the rest of his classmates, who hunched over his desk with a big scowl on his face, softly, but noticeably tapping the desk with his pencil in an unrelenting staccato rhythm. He was easy to figure, but the isolation booth occupant on the other side of the room was a beautiful little girl with the sweetest face imaginable, framed by a mop of soft reddish blond ringlets. She looked ready-made to sit on a shelf at Toys-R-Us, staring out at eager shoppers with big blue endearing eyes that said, "Take me home." What crimes had one so seemingly angelic committed, I wondered.

Mrs. Jennings (I never learned her first name) interrupted my reverie, approaching me gingerly to ask if I would take the day's lunch order to the cafeteria. "Sure," I said, perhaps too readily.

Apparently, she was emboldened by my quick response. My next chore was running off copies for the day's lessons. I didn't really mind that because I knew from my first two days of substituting how difficult it is to find time to make those preparations. Unless you are prepared to arrive very early (which I did) or give up lunch (half an hour), there are few opportunities for prep work. So I resolved to fully earn my keep for this one day in a role that I had not anticipated. But before my tour of duty ended, I had peeled potatoes, strung beads, made cutouts, dispensed glue and glitter, done recess duty, escorted little people to the rest room and run various additional errands.

It was the holiday season. Mrs. Jennings read a Hanukkah story to the children. While they sat on an area rug in a cozy semi-circle expanding their cultural horizons, I would guess that I peeled ten pounds or more of spuds for the traditional potato pancakes with which the lesson would culminate.

I had never peeled so many potatoes at one sitting in my entire life—not for family celebrations, reunions, anything! And believe you me, if you have ever wielded a not-very-sharp potato peeler that many times, you'd remember. Of course they didn't eat them; they were served up after lunch and nobody was hungry even though the whole kindergarten corridor was blanketed with the enticing smell of fried potatoes.

As I cleaned up the mess and dumped the peels, I breathed a well-earned sigh of relief because the worst of this particular assignment was obviously over. We were one and a half hours away from dismissal.

But, as it developed, I sighed too soon. In this land of equal opportunity—and from where I sat, equal misery—we were not finished. Next we had to do something for the Christians. Out came the string, beads, construction paper, glue and glitter. In the last period of the day, we were going to make Christmas tree ornaments.

Yes, I reassured myself throughout the day, I can peel potatoes, I can string beads, I am a secure person, and I know who I am. Therefore, I resolved to be the best-damned potato peeler and bead stringer anybody could ask for. But let's be clear; I'm not masochistic. I would return the next day to complete this two-day assignment, but beyond that, I wouldn't do it again. It wasn't about an ego thing. It just wasn't what I was hired to do, and I require a bit more creativity at the workplace than my potato peeling day had afforded.

Rule 4: Beware of parapro power.

In the school system, paraprofessionals are neither fish nor fowl. They're not quite professional but they're not administrative either. Actually, the administrative staff wields considerably more weight. Everybody in the system recognizes that school secretaries and clerks have the big bosses' ears. Mess with them and they can mess you up royally, whispering all kinds of negative little nothings to the powers that be, which could spell your eventual demise. And, of course, they make more money than subs. But then, so does everybody else, except the parapros.

From what I observed, parapros barely measure a cut above custodial and cafeteria staff on the respect Richter. Understandably, they have an image problem. So who are they gonna dump on? Straight case, substitutes. Subs are the only staff in the system without union protection or community advocates.

Attitudinally, I found paras the most pompous of all the school's personnel. They greeted me with a suspicious eye that said, "If you were worth your salt, you'd have a regular classroom assignment, even if you aren't yet eligible for certification." Of course, let them tell it, they had opted to be housewives and didn't take their jobs for the money. The justifications: "My kids are in this school and the job affords me an opportunity to monitor their progress and hold the teachers accountable"; "I'm dealing with the 'empty nest' syndrome and need something to keep me from going stir crazy"; "My husband's work requires long hours and lots of travel and this is a good antidote for my shopping addiction."

Well, as I said, through some assignment confusion, I found myself for two days not a substitute teacher but a substitute parapro! Does it get any tougher than that? Boy, did I catch it! The regulars hardly spoke to me at all, except to apprise me of my designated duties. Of course, it was my turn for everything, from morning bus to cafeteria to recess to dismissal duty.

How could I argue? I didn't know the schedule and the classroom teacher, who was inventing my role hour by hour as the day progressed with every menial task within her purview, could hardly be expected to come to my rescue. Appealing to the administration would be futile, I surmised. Four days in the school and I hadn't a clue who ran the place. No authority figure had been introduced; the school secretary doled out the assignments. And I wouldn't have attempted an appeal anyway, even if I had known to whom such an appeal should be addressed. Parapros are permanent staff; subs are transients. Paras have roots in the community (PTA and PTO members) and their own grassroots sphere of influence. In a dispute, whose side is the principal going to come down on? I'm told they're reluctant to even defend their own teachers in paraprofessional conflicts, so, obviously, subs don't stand a chance. Confronted with these realities, I swallowed my battered pride and meekly did as I was told.

Cafeteria duty wasn't so bad. Mostly, I just walked around looking officious, telling some overly animated kids to lower their voices, clean up their tables and return their trays. It was in this role that I heard the first kind paraprofessional voice.

"Hi. My name is Jamie," said the smiling face.

I was so surprised by this simple act of kindness that I became suddenly mute, dumbly searching for my voice.

"I'm Barbara," I said gratefully when I was able to speak.

"Are you a new parapro?" asked Jamie.

"No, uh, no," I said hesitantly, while I regained my identity. "I'm a substitute teacher. This is my first assignment."

"Whadya doing here?" she asked, her face registering surprise. "Teachers don't do lunch duty."

"I don't know," I said. "There's some kind of mix-up and they have me subbing for a parapro today."

"Well, you just be careful," Jamie cautioned. "Don't let them push you around. They'll try it, you know. They always try to dump on the new people."

I later discovered that Jamie was the lunchroom supervisor. She stood out in a crowd as the one in charge. It helped that she was a big woman: tall and stately, big-boned, with an equally big heart. But one recognized immediately that she was no pushover; someone who didn't take stuff. It was apparent that both the kids and the other parapros routinely shrank beneath her towering presence.

For me, it was love at first sight. Jamie was at once my friend, my sister, my savior. From that day on, she was my go-to person whenever I was in a muddle. Thanks to her, I started to get a handle on what subs were and weren't supposed to do.

On my first day of recess duty it was unseasonably, bone-chilling cold. I hadn't dressed properly. Sunny days in the South can be deceptive in the late fall, and I had only prepared to go from my car to the building. Wrapping myself as best I could in my inadequate little leather jacket, I stood scrunched up with chattering teeth watching a parade of thoroughly wired little classroom escapees go absolutely berserk in the makeshift playground. This school was in its first year of operation, so a number of construction jobs, including a playground, were still pending.

The provisional playground was a vacant lot adjacent to the fenced in parking lot. Stubby little patches of grass and weeds dotted a barren, dismal spread of red Georgia clay dirt. Standard playground fixtures were yet to be installed. There were no organized games and no equipment. It was just a place where the kids could run around in aimless frenetic circles and release some pent up energy.

Twenty minutes can be an eternity when the blood is freezing in your veins and your hands are turning blue. I observed the children at play with as much attention as I could muster in my near frozen state. There wasn't much to see. The games that they devised seemed to have no identifiable goals. My job, I surmised, was primarily to stand guard and make sure that nobody killed anybody while they exhausted themselves before returning to the classroom somewhat subdued for the afternoon session.

I was pretty passive at first, taking my directions from assertive paras in stride. But ultimately, I drew the line. On my second day as Mrs. Jennings' parapro, there was a cold misting, penetrating rain, but recess had not been canceled.

"Come on," I heard the command as I huddled just inside the double doors peering out at a dismal unsheltered wasteland. "You have to go to your post," my self-appointed supervisor announced, brusquely sweeping the door open before me.

A little lady, dwarfed in stature, stood in front of me wrapped in a somewhat frayed heavy winter coat with a wool scarf swerved tightly around her neck and a black striped knit cap pulled down over her ears hiding everything but her little round red bubble of a face and glaring red-rimmed eyes. I had to suppress a laugh. Looking at her, I could hear the refrain of an old song from yesteryear reverberating in my brain: "Mr. Five by Five, five feet tall and five feet wide..."

"Come on," she repeated raising her voice and sharpening her tone to jolt me out of my reverie. "You have to go to your post! You're supposed to be standing at the far end of the parking lot, you know," she barked, pointing in the direction of the parked cars.

I stared back at her, not moving. She was a familiar sight. I had seen her in so many other settings. She was the prototypical schoolyard pariah who had learned long ago how to get her bluff in first. Well, this was the wrong day to push me around. Normally somewhat acquiescent, I was too cold that day to care about consequences.

You see, I have this rule of thumb: Know when to hold, when to fold, and when to just say no. There was no way that I, being particularly susceptible to the vagaries of inclement weather in my second half century, was going to risk my death shivering in a freezing rain doing recess duty. So, I just said no.

My thoughts: Fire me, never hire me again, but I am not going out there this day so inadequately prepared. My voice was deep, exacting and controlled as I stated my refusal. Apparently my face said it all. Girlfriend looked stunned for a moment, obviously not anticipating that response. Her face registered multiple shades of crimson as she contemplated the situation and then decided to back off. After that encounter, she never attempted to supervise my performance again.

She never spoke to me again either, but that was fine. There are some greetings I can live without.

Rule 5: Make friends with monsters, ink

Of course it's easier to like the students who like and accept you, but remember, you've got to teach the whole class, not just your "special" new friends. As you might suspect, it's often the ones who go out of their way to alienate you who are most in need of some attention. And whatever you do, don't just ignore them, because distance will only fuel their hostilities.

Who are the little monsters that can make your day a living nightmare? I repeat, your first clue is the seating arrangement. They are usually boys: the boy whose desk has been moved next to the teacher's or the two who occupy the "isolation booths" at the far corners of the room.

It is to your advantage and theirs that you don't know anybody's history. You'll find out soon enough who's who, but initially everybody gets a chance to start off with a clean slate. If neighboring teachers insist on pointing out the usual suspects, try to remain objective in your treatment of them.

Now, I'm not bragging, but I kinda have a way with kids. Across the age spectrum, they generally like me, especially the young ones. In my family I'm known as the Pied Piper of all the small children. Even at church when I'm dressed in my Sunday best, drooling babies have a way of leaping into my arms. I attribute this natural rapport in part to my own psyche, a portion of which must be frozen somewhere in perpetual childhood. So, I've always found it reasonably easy to get inside young people's heads and communicate on their level.

After my first week at Middle Town, as I said, I had acquired several new best friends in the fifth and second grades where I had substituted. Second graders are particularly affectionate. They tend to be inordinately touchy-feely but, unfortunately, in today's world, we adults aren't allowed to respond. My heart was particularly warmed by little Jake, a pint-sized second grader who would do most anything for a little attention, including sprawling flat on the floor in a snow angel kind of posture directly in the path of classmates who had learned to ignore him and simply stepped around him.

Every time Jake got within striking distance, he would stroke my arm or reach out to grab my hand or attempt to plant a kiss. "Give me a hug," he entreated, with big doleful eyes that cried out for affection. I didn't. I had been told we couldn't. Rules are rules and we were sternly admonished not to touch *them*. But I must confess that I didn't really resist when he would creep up behind me with a surprise smack attack.

So I wasn't really intimated by Toby and Dawson, the so-called toughs in the fifth grade.

Toby was a slow learner. There are all kinds of euphemistic ways of saying it nowadays, i.e. Early Intervention Program (EIP), intellectually challenged, but in plain English, he was simply a slow learner. And his peers punished him for it.

"He doesn't read with us," they chorused as if *he* wasn't there. "He goes to Mr. Blake for math," they were quick to point out. Toby just scowled and kicked his desk. Tall and gangly, he had a way of scrunching down into his seat as if attempting to make himself invisible.

My informants did a good job of telling me everything Toby couldn't do, so my challenge was to find out what he could do. I discovered that he liked to color and could be quite meticulous with charts and diagrams. So when I expressed my appreciation for his talent and held his work up as an example for all to see, he beamed, unable to suppress what was really a beautiful, if mostly hidden, smile. When he brought his next creation to my attention, anxiously awaiting my approval, I knew I had made a friend.

The fifth graders confirmed my belief that rewards work better than punishment. It helped that these students liked their teacher and wanted a good report. So I kept on the board for all to see a "Most Cooperative" list to be presented to Mrs. Kane when she returned.

Every day, Toby would ask me before dismissal if he had been good enough to make the cut. He would even sit for short periods--as long as he could endure the discipline-- with hands folded on his desk, eyes following me beseechingly around the room to see if I was noticing. I thought he would burst with pride when, with a considerable stretch of my imagination, I wrote his name on the big rewards board. Never mind that it only meant a piece of candy or some extra time in one of the room's interest centers, you'd have thought he'd won the lottery.

I even allowed Toby to lead the line. It was probably one of the few, if any, leadership roles he had ever assumed in his entire life. Yes, it was shameless co-optation on my part, but it worked. And it was certainly better to have him in full view at the front of the line than in his usual rear flank position sparring with his classmates. My definition of a win-win.

I repeat, I can take only so much credit for the smooth sailing I enjoyed with the fifth graders. Reading Mrs. Kane's lesson plans, it was easy to understand why her class was so manageable. Her assumption was that productive work would take place in her absence. A prescription for busy work it was not.

She obviously was a very good teacher, evidenced by the behavior and attitudes of her students toward learning. Being on her "good list" was important to them.

By the end of my first week, I had more "best friends" than I knew what to do with. Toby, the biggest threat initially, turned out to be a paper tiger, and once he came over to my side, Dawson and the other would-be defiant ones just kind of caved in.

The other teachers in the cluster repeatedly congratulated me. "They were so quiet," they marveled. "How did you do it?"

"Mrs. Kane left a very good plan," I said modestly. I could afford to be generous. It had been a great week.

Ms. Crawley's third graders were a different story. I had thought this would be my most rewarding assignment since this was the

grade I had always preferred in my early teaching years. Was I ever wrong! It didn't take me long to realize that this class would be one tough nut to crack. I knew it even before I was told about their teacher's contempt for them ("She bolts through the door snorting, 'I hate them! I just hate them'") and before I could make my own assessment of the cast of characters ("Jude is a sad case. He was born to a drug addicted mother and he's so out of it most of the time until he completely loses it and totally goes off").

They didn't come in and get down to business like the other classes I had been teaching. Instead, they'd stroll around the room from one end to the other, laughing and cavorting, finishing their breakfast while trading stories and treats. Although I stood at the door greeting them as they arrived, they took little notice of me except to try and run game: "I've got to go to the library now to take these books back." "I have my baby sister's coloring book and she's gonna need it." "I have to go to the nurse because I have a cold." "I've gotta go to the bathroom—really bad." All the old excuses I had ever heard for getting out of the classroom and even some new ones.

They had the most wretched work habits of any class I had ever seen, past or present. This class was right out of the old "blackboard jungle" movie genre, the kind that makes you say, "Oh please! This is so over the top, like too contrived." They sailed paper missiles across the room. Like a room full of jumping jacks, they bolted out of their seats every few seconds to the pencil sharpener or wastebasket, or simply to boldly visit with a classmate on the other side of the room. I knew immediately that bringing some order and discipline to this bedlam would be a monumental challenge.

The first few days were trial by fire. But, because I am far too vain to think of myself as a babysitter or a quitter, with some trepidation I took up the mantle. I'm a teacher, I told myself, and teach I will.

My first challenge was to get the class on my side. I kept reminding myself that, no matter what their history, most of them really do want to learn. So my best defense was to engage them in meaningful learning activities. Reaching deeply into my arsenal of child pleasers, I began to devise a plan.

Lest you think me too heroic, I must confess that my efforts weren't altogether altruistic. It was also very much a matter of my own survival. There was simply no way I could get out of my bed in the morning and drive some 45 minutes to work to face unmitigated chaos. A martyr I am not. Thus, we had to come to some kind of understanding for our mutual benefit.

Pardon the cliché, but I really believe that honesty is the best policy for children of all ages. Children are generally far savvier than we may be inclined to think. They understood, for instance, that I was temporary (their teacher was out on medical leave having foot surgery) and that ultimately it would not be I who would decide whether they passed on to the next grade or got left back. So why should they be accountable to me in her absence?

Well, I laid it on the line for them: "I'll be here for at least three weeks, maybe longer. Now, I, or pretty much any substitute who comes after me, will get paid whether we teach you anything or not. You have to make a decision. If I close the door and read magazines all day while you do pretty much as you please, including going berserk from time to time, who's the big loser? I have more than one college degree, but you're trying to get to the next grade and improve your learning skills along the way. And if you're successful, you too can go to college some day. So what's it going to be? Do I get paid to do nothing or do I earn my pay by teaching you important lessons you need to learn to pass on to the next grade?"

The good news is that most kids can be reasoned with. The inclination to grow intellectually is perhaps as natural as physical or any other kind of development. Spend some time with precocious three-year-olds and before you can show them how to do anything, they're likely to smugly declare their independence, asserting, "I can do it." And simplistic as it sounds, we know that the brain, like the body, must be fed our entire life.

My granddaughter, at age three wanted to tie her shoe laces, button her clothes, comb her own hair, and even wrestle the nutcracker from me when I was opening walnuts. Although this natural propensity may have been battered and bruised by the time some children reach the third grade, we can still use it to our advantage.

The first thing we did was clean up the place. The room was a mess. This was a new school in its first year, but you wouldn't know it from the looks of the wreckage that was this particular classroom. Desks were brimming over with an assorted clutter of notebooks, backpacks, sweaters, jackets, crayons, water bottles, soda cans, lunch boxes, loose papers and other debris that spilled over onto the floor making it virtually impossible for the custodian to vacuum the fully carpeted classroom at day's end. This was in sharp contrast to the other rooms in the cluster where children neatly stacked their chairs on top of their cleanly scrubbed desks at the end of each school day.

Well, they needed to know that their room was an embarrassment to their teacher, their school and their parents. It neither looked nor felt like a good place to study, so we were going to do something about that. We would start by cleaning up our desks. The teacher's desk, incidentally, was nearly as disorganized at the students'.

This Herculean task consumed a large part of the first day. The custodian was delighted to accommodate us with a generous supply of large trash bags. By the time the dismissal bell rang, there were no more spillovers on the floor and desks were nearly all cleared. Their floor, for the first time in recent memory, I was told by the custodial staff, could be thoroughly cleaned like others in the school.

Bit by bit the point was made: coats, sweaters, backpacks go in the closet area, and whatever doesn't fit in desks had to be removed at the end of the day. I sensed a new pride permeating the occupants of our cleaner, more organized environment. Over the next several days they learned to raise their hands before speaking, request permission before leaving their seats and sharpen pencils when entering the classroom in the morning and after lunch. I think little Ken summed up the feelings of the majority of his classmates when he whispered in my ear, "Miss Miles, I like the way you're making us clean up this place," and on another occasion, "I like the way you're making us behave ourselves." It underscored what I've always believed: children like and need structure in their lives as much as we adults.

Don't be fooled when children laugh and egg on the class clowns. In reality, they also like order and can be persuaded to see themselves as the losers when the clowns' antics bring learning activities to a screeching halt. One day, I decided to confront the disruptives head-on in a non-confrontational manner.

My approach was to present the problem to the whole class and invite their suggestions for dealing with it. I told them a story about my youngest granddaughter, who one day was very put out by something her older sister, Kara, had done. Thoroughly aggravated, she sat in a corner of the room frantically dialing on a toy telephone.

"Who are you calling?" I asked. She was so engrossed in this activity that at first she didn't respond. I repeated the question.

"I'm talling the police," she replied.

"Why are you calling the police," I probed.

"I'm talling the police to tome pick up Karwa."

I had their attention. When they finished laughing, they pretended to dial imaginary phones and call the police to come pick up Dak, a chronic troublemaker.

"Well, Kelsey was only three, so she thought calling the police on her sister was the solution to her problem," I said. "But we're all old enough to know that calling the police will not solve our problems here in the classroom."

I listened to their draconian suggestions—from sending the boy to the principal's office to calling his parents to expelling him—before intervening. When it was time to come to Dak's rescue, I began by explaining, "Dak really is a very bright boy. He likes lots of attention, but he just has to realize that there are good ways and there are bad ways to make us notice him. He can be one of the best students in this class any time he makes up his mind to stop clowning around and get down to the serious business of learning."

"Yeah, Dak, why don't you just cut out the clowning," they scolded.

"Well, Dak, how about it?" I asked.

"Okay," he said. "I'll cut it out. I promise."

And he did, at least for a while. I continually encouraged him academically and looked for opportunities to give him the attention he so desperately needed, but for his successes rather than his comedic antics.

Rule 6: Master the name game.

What's in a name? Well, Shakespeare, I'm here to tell you, a helluva lot. And the names of today's kids will boggle the best minds...and tongues.

But remember, children like their names, odd spellings and tongue twisters notwithstanding. It is undoubtedly one thing in this universe of uncertainties that they own; that has always belonged to them. They don't know the world I grew up in; a world of Johns, Marys, Williams, Elizabeths and Susans. If there's a Christy, it's likely to begin with a K and end with an i, and Tyler may well be a girl. Shenequas, Jamillahs and Queenitas are as common now as Henry, George and Carol were in my school days.

I reiterate, however creative and complex the spellings, they know their names; their classmates know their names; their friends, family members and teachers know their names, so why should subs be any exception? They expect us to get it right, and when we don't, they're offended.

Before entering your classroom, it might behoove you to do a little research. If you have friends in the system, ask if you can sneak a peek at their class rosters. Attend the graduations and peruse the class lists of young relatives in ethnically diverse schools. Examine any rosters at your disposal for designer names and get help with the pronunciations. It will stand you in good stead if names like Chimeryia, DeMarkantoneus and Voneisha roll easily off your tongue before you begin your first assignment.

Arrive early if possible, read the class roll and practice saying the more challenging names. But as subs know well, many assignments come the same day and the kids may well be there when you arrive. Worst case scenario: you enter the classroom ten minutes or more after the morning session has begun to find the children already seated with a parapro holding down the fort, impatiently fidgeting while awaiting your arrival. You walk in; she mumbles something vaguely resembling a greeting and walks out.

And there you are, face-to-face with a roomful of strangers critically monitoring your every move. What to do?

Start by introducing yourself; write *your* name on the board. Don't attempt to call the roll right away. The first thing you need to do is engage them in some meaningful activity.

Morning work generally does not introduce new skills but reinforces lessons previously taught. If the teacher expected to be out, he/she may have left morning work on the board the previous day. If the boards are blank, locate the lesson plan. Most schools require teachers to leave at least a full day's plan within the substitute's easy reach. Can't find a lesson plan? Enlist the children in the search. They are usually pretty adept at tracking down plan books along with any other books or supplies you can't readily locate.

But remember, your class can't just sit idle while you turn your back on them to write assignments on the board. Give them something to do while you're organizing the morning lessons. If you know what grade you'll be teaching, think of a "story starter" while traveling to the school, just in case. If the teacher has a story starter in her plan, use hers. If not, introduce your own.

Write the beginning sentence or sentences for the story on the board and explain the assignment. You may want to have them share related experiences or ideas to make sure everybody knows what's expected of them. Once they are busy writing, you can put up additional work and then take a few minutes to prepare for the name game.

If there's a seating chart, you can take attendance without calling the roll. Often names are also on their desks. Then, you can walk quietly around the room while they're writing and see who's missing. This is also a good way to check pronunciations. If in doubt, quietly ask students individually how they say their names.

If you have neither of these luxuries at your disposal, you're probably going to have to bite the bullet and call the roll. Again, honesty is the best policy. Admit that you may need help pronouncing some of their names. Then when you come to the showstoppers, ask if it's Chi-me-ree-a or Chi-meer-e-a. Yes, they'll still laugh at you when you get it wrong, but I found it helpful to laugh with them and graciously accept their help. They always find it a bit of a coup to be able to teach the teacher.

Rule 7: Know who's who and what's what.

I will tell you this story as it unfolded and allow you to draw your own conclusions. I'll preface it by explaining that while on recess duty certain kids with whom I'd had no prior interaction tended to catch my eye. It might have been a smile, exceptional good looks or a mode of dress that made them stand out in a crowd. Thus, there were several kids that I knew by sight who, for some reason, had made a memorable impression. In this category, Tonequa stood out.

He was the consummate hip-hopster from head to toe. Start with the hair, worn in cornrows queuing up neatly at the nape of his neck a la popular rock stars and revered sports heroes. His broad distinctive facial features were familiar, yet uniquely different. But it was his style of dress that really defined him. Everything was oversized; each day there was a different shirt that was four or more sizes too big draped over gargantuan denim trousers that sagged well below his waist and gathered in jumbled layers over sneakers with thick, chunky soles raised three or more inches from the floor.

The walk was consistent with the dress. I can only describe it as the hip-hop shuffle that is the essence of cool in some urban inner city neighborhoods. That, I thought, watching Tonequa prance down the hall with a measured rhythm in every step, is one cool cat.

Imagine my surprise when Tonequa (his classmates called him Tony) turned up in my fifth grade classroom. Suddenly, I had a name for Mister Cool and the name seemed a perfect fit.

Unduly influenced by stereotypes, I initially thought he might spell trouble. As it turned out, Tonequa was one of the nicest kids in the class. Always polite, he never spoke out without raising his hand, finished his work on time, busied himself productively in one of the interest centers when he had spare time and never gave me an ounce of grief. He was soft-spoken and always cooperative. That's why I couldn't believe my lying eyes when I walked into the girls' restroom one day during morning break to chase out the stragglers and saw none other than Tonequa standing in the middle of a group of his classmates chatting unabashedly as if being there was the most natural thing in the world.

I was shocked. I felt betrayed. I had been had. This was not the nice kid I had taken him for. He had played me royally, pretending to pose no threat while positioning himself all along to take me down for all to see. I was stunned; I was hurt; I was angry. And most of all, I was afraid. What was I supposed to do in this situation? I doubt if any manual had ever covered this type of circumstance. What if I got it wrong? It would surely be my undoing.

Somewhere, in the deepest depression of my throat, I found a remnant of my voice and uttered the only word I could muster. "Out!" I said emphatically, pointing to the door. I hoped I sounded authoritative; that my normally soft voice had a decided edge that said I meant business. I may be a sub, I thought, but if it's a showdown he wants, a showdown he will get.

"Out!" I said again, more forcefully this time when he failed to respond. It had to be abundantly clear that his immediate exit was non-negotiable.

"What did I do?" he asked, looking me dead straight in the eye and feigning innocence.

"Don't even try it," I retorted. My voice was getting edgier by the minute. Onlookers stood frozen in their tracks. This was a side of me they had not seen. But the battle line was drawn.

"But what did I do?" he had the unmitigated gall to ask again.

This time I didn't reply. I simply stood my ground, edging closer to get in his face, and kept pointing to the door. Panic was nibbling at the fringes of my bravado, but I couldn't show it. What if he didn't go? I hadn't plotted my next move.

But I didn't blink. Kids are quick to smell fear. "I want you out of here right now, and I don't intend to tell you again," I said in an even measured tone that belied my rising anxiety.

He shrugged, apparently surrendering. "But my hands are wet," he said, making one last futile attempt to get over on me.

I didn't answer. I had said all I intended to say. I simply stared him through the door.

Once I had gotten him into the hallway and regained my composure, I noticed that his hands were dripping wet and he was attempting to dry them on his clothes. In a somewhat conciliatory gesture, I pointed to the boys' restroom and said, "Now stop clowning around and go in there and dry your hands."

There was a pregnant pause followed by a palpable silence. The other children, forming a line in the hallway while waiting for the dawdlers, were momentarily transfixed before grasping the full measure of my colossal gaffe.

Then came the horrible pronouncement: "She's a girl," they chorused in unison to my startled ears. "Tonequa's a girl, Miss Miles."

Oh my God! Oh dear God, what had I done? Would the floor just open up and swallow me whole. What had I done to poor Tonequa?

Think fast! I commanded my paralyzed brain. Angel of the Lord, somebody, anybody, rescue me from this abyss into which I'm rapidly sinking.

"Ha, ha, ha," the children's voices bounced off the ceiling and walls as the hallway exploded with laughter. Even now, if I close my eyes I can still hear them. "Miss Miles thought Toni was a boy," they said again and again, slapping themselves and each other in uncontrollable mirth.

Mercifully, there is a God. In my confusion I spied one of those athlete's headbands around Tonequa's neatly coifed cornrows. That would have to be the explanation for my catastrophic mistake.

"Girl, take that headband off your head and go on back in there and dry your hands," I scolded, this time pointing to the girls' room. "No wonder I didn't recognize you."

"We're not supposed to wear headbands in class," one boy volunteered, inadvertently bailing me out. The laughing stopped.

Apparently, they had accepted my lame excuse for the awful blunder. But I couldn't just leave it there. I owed Tonequa and the class more than that.

"I'm so embarrassed," I confessed when she was safely out of sight. "Did you ever do something that was really stupid?" I asked of no one in particular. I felt the need to make myself the butt of this wretched joke.

Luckily, there were plenty of volunteers coming forward to share their stupid stories. Soon they were so engrossed in their own tales that they forgot the origin of this digression. When Tonequa returned to the line, nobody took any special notice of her nor treated her any differently.

But my head was spinning and couldn't let it go. What if she had been a boy? Transgender? How does the school treat restroom breaks for those children? Is there some protocol that I should have known about? Certainly, it was not included in the list of "40 Things Every Substitute Should Know" that was given to us in the orientation session.

I won't bore you with a bunch of platitudes gleaned from this experience. My lesson was a simple one: Know what you're talking about before you open your big fat stupid mouth and put your foot in it.

ARE YOU MARRIED?
DO YOU DYE YOUR HAIR?
ARE THESE EXTENSIONS
ARE THESE YOUR REAL NAILS?

Rule 8: Don't take it personally.

Be prepared; they'll want to know your whole history. The better they like you, the more they'll prod you for personal information. "Are you married?" "Do you dye your hair?" "Do you have extensions?" "Are those your real nails?" And those are just the warm-ups.

But the most persistent and nagging question was this: "How old are you?" Can anybody of my generation even remotely imagine any classmate having the gall to confront a teacher with such personal questions when we were in elementary school? They were grownups and teachers; that was all we needed to know.

And don't let the colorist miss the mark with hair treatment. Be prepared for such probes as: "Why is your hair streaked yellowish?" and "Is your natural hair color gray?" Catch the wrong ray of light and the question becomes: "Did you intend to dye your hair green?"

But ever and always they'd come back to the age question. Obviously, they are programmed to be age conscious much earlier these days. Almost every day a different delegation of fifth graders confronted me: "Please, please tell us; how old are you?"

"Do you have a need to know?" I playfully stonewalled them, borrowing a tenet from the federal government's requirement for sharing classified information.

"Yes," they insisted. "Yes, we need to know. Why won't you tell us?" They were unrelenting.

"Because it's personal, and you really don't need to know." End of story? Not really.

As a general rule, I don't tell my age. Where I come from, friends don't ask and it's nobody else's business. And if I hadn't divulged my confidential data to the inquiring minds of new southern best friends, why should I give it up to monsters, ink?

Another reason for my reticence is that people generally take me to be younger than I am. Some undiscerning strangers would still ask if my daughter and I were sisters and if my son was my husband. And

I must confess, I didn't mind that a bit. If someone wanted to pare my number down by twenty or so years, hey, I don't have a problem with it. After all, wasn't preservation what all those years of healthy diets and exercise were about?

That said, you can imagine my chagrin when the leader of the band smugly announced one morning, "I already know how old you are."

She had my attention. Gretchen was the senior citizen of the class and as such the uncontested sage. She had been left back a couple of times, not because she wasn't smart or even so much that she was lazy, but more likely because of her defiant attitude. I suspect she could have performed better on standardized tests if she had been persuaded they would yield her some tangible benefit. Passing on to the next grade was apparently not a big enough incentive.

"Oh you do, do you?" I challenged. "And just how old am I?"

"You're fifty," she said without hesitation. As far as she was concerned, it was case closed.

"Fifty!" I feigned a gasp. It was a surprisingly big number for a child, especially inasmuch as forty is old to them at their age. But this worldly-wise pundit was letting me know that I wasn't putting anything over on her. My curiosity was aroused.

"What makes you think I'm fifty?" I probed.

"Well, you ain't forty," she said decisively. Then came the coup de grace: "I'm looking at yo' face."

Well, I was busted. What could I say? At least she hadn't said sixty. But there was more to come.

Gretchen's declaration seemed to settle the age issue for the fifth graders. Okay, I consoled myself. They can figure these things out. I talk a lot about my grandkids. Their parents are mostly in their thirties, some maybe early forties. I was older than they. Ergo, I must be fifty. Score one for deductive reasoning.

I had imagined the third graders would be less intrusive. Indeed, I don't recall any of them just asking me my age outright. But when the blow came from that quarter, it was considerably more savage.

It was only in that third grade class that I was occasionally driven to a complete loss of my cool. Unlike the other classes that I taught at Middle Town, they had been conditioned by their teacher to respond to ugly faces and loud yelling. It was a condition I had inherited and loathed. But, occasionally, it was only that kind of shock treatment that got their attention and succeeded in restoring order.

Such was the case one day when, in total frustration, I stood in the middle of the room and let loose. It worked momentarily. The class obviously was stunned because yelling was generally out of character for me. The proverbial pin drop could be heard during the long pregnant pause that followed my outburst. But before I could regroup and restart the lesson, there was discernible mumbling under the breath of one of the bolder, more fearless instigators.

"You oughta see how yo face looks when you do that," said Chantay. "You look like a big ole ugly go-rilla."

I was speechless; Rip Van Winkle waking to a world I no longer recognized. Where had these children come from? When had the classroom become such a mean and hostile place where students felt free to assault their teacher with ugly name-calling? I wondered how many teachers endeavored to educate on a day-to-day basis in this kind of atmosphere. And whom should we blame? Parents? Teachers? Administrators? The culture? All of the above?

"I can't do this," I thought. Not with this group, anyway. Maybe I'm too emotionally fragile; I care too much. They'll have me back in therapy where I had sought refuge for two solid years while going through my last painfully acrimonious divorce. Nothing was worth that. Certainly, my three hours of orientation had not prepared me for this.

Dak saw opportunity and quickly weighed in. "Yeah," he said. "Miss Miles may look like a diva, but she's old."

.aybe he was right. Maybe I just didn't have the stamina for this ⅃ of punishment at this stage of my life. He had struck a nerve.

At that moment, I just wanted to pick up my bag, storm out of the room, get into my car and drive away. But I didn't. A small voice inside my head said, "Remember, you're the adult in the room, the enforcer of a new discipline so that makes you the enemy right now. They're only children; don't take it personally."

Rule 9: Prepare for germ warfare.

Never mind my bruised ego; I had no time to brood. There were bigger issues to confront. The job should have come with a warning: *Substitute teaching can be hazardous to your health.*

Each day, as I pulled out tissues, hand wipes and various other items from my defense arsenal, I'd chuckle to myself, recalling a little jingle from my childhood: *At ease disease; there's a fungus among us.* That old saying had never seemed more appropriate.

It's no secret that children are notorious germ carriers. And as everybody who knows me knows, I am particularly susceptible to any and everybody else's germs. If somebody's spreading it, I'm catching it. The joke when I go home to New York to see the grandkids is that two doses of disease come with every love hug.

So I entered the classroom with a fair amount of trepidation. Yes, I'd had my flu and pneumonia shots. Yes, my tetanus immunization was still current. But how do you defend against the most prevalent menace of all: the common cold?

I had started this bold journey at the height of the cold and flu season, so there was no time to build immunity to threats in my new environment before the siege. They came at me full throttle from day one. Almost immediately, I found myself drowning in a sea of coughs, sniffles and runny noses. Inspector Clouseau's admonition of Pink Panther fame echoed in my brain: "Touch nothing!"

Ha! Teaching, I soon discovered, is a contact sport. You can't touch a desk, pick up an eraser, or open a door without risking contagion. You could go in with a moon suit and they'd still get to you. Disease was everywhere. Taylor had a pink eye. Darcel had a chronic nosebleed and thoroughly bloody tissues to prove it. Steve had been hospitalized for several days with pneumonia but because his parents didn't want him to miss school any longer, his doctor was persuaded to allow him to return to class and I was charged with monitoring his progress. If he showed any signs of relapse, he might have to be re-admitted. It seemed hardly an hour went by without someone requesting permission to go to the health center. With so many legitimate problems, it was hard to tell who was faking.

I'm being *pranked*, I thought. Is this a reality show or what? There really can't be this many ailing children in one classroom.

Just before the Christmas holiday break, the first telltale signs started to creep up on me; the scratchy throat, the sneezing, the tearing eyes. When time came for me to pack for my annual New York holiday visit, I was also packing one of the nastiest colds I had experienced in recent memory. My only consolation was that this time I wouldn't have to dodge the grand's germ bullets. For once, I would be turning the tables and taking it to them.

So, my educated advice is this: Don't mess around! Get your flu shots; take your vitamins and any other preventive therapies available to fortify yourself. Otherwise, you may end up spending more on doctor bills than you earn.

Remember, there are no paid leave or health benefits for substitutes. If you catch it, you own it; it's yours to nurse and cure and pay for. And yes, you guessed it; there are no death benefits either.

ARE YOU AN ADMINISTRATOR?
ARE THERE ANY DISCIPLINARY GUIDELINES?

Rule 10: Speak when spoken to.

Except for neighboring teachers, there was no support; not even for simple things like getting a few urgent supplies. The felt markers left by Mrs. Crawley for writing on the whiteboard were all dried out. I asked at the office, and no one could find even one or two to get me started. All I ever got was an exhaustive procedure for ordering supplies. Fortunately, Mrs. Allen, the teacher across the hall, came to my rescue.

The school day started at 8 o'clock. Teachers were expected to sign in by 7:45. I arrived every day between 7:00 and 7:15. I was always the first sub to sign in. Usually only the secretarial, custodial and cafeteria staff beat me in. Whether I was following somebody else's lesson plan or generating my own, I needed some time to get my bearings and structure my day before the children arrived.

It helped that I happen to be an early riser. Thanks in part to chronic insomnia, a carryover from my publishing days when I was forever plagued by pressing deadlines, I was usually up before the alarm sounded. And as you might surmise, I was on my feet practically the whole day. Thoroughly exhausted by day's end, the closing bell was music to my ears.

Dismissal started at 3:15. On good days, the kids would all be called for their buses by 3:45. As they straggled out in twos and threes, I struggled to keep the late pick-ups entertained. It was just my luck, it seemed, that the most difficult students were the last ones called. On my very first day, as I was overseeing the tidying of desks and floors before dismissal, the door suddenly burst open. To my bewildered eyes, in walked Mr. Martin, a teacher down the hall, with another 20-plus kids in tow.

"What the f____!" I mumbled under my breath, almost cursing out loud. As I stood speechless watching this ambush, he announced that it was my turn for dismissal duty, then beat a hasty retreat. My resilience was sorely tested, but somehow I got through it.

If I didn't already know that I was out there on my own, a brief encounter in the cafeteria during my first week brought it home. I had noticed a certain woman pacing the adjacent hallway and occasionally walking through the cafeteria. This person wasn't dressed like a parapro, and she wasn't dressed like the other teachers either. She always wore well coordinated business attire: suits or tailored jackets, modest heels and stockings. Judging from her dress, I concluded that she must be someone in a position of authority. Maybe she could answer a few questions for me about school procedures.

I approached her one day after I dropped the children off for lunch, thinking this would be an opportune time to talk to someone who could point me in the direction of some much needed help. "Are you an administrator?" I asked.

"Yes," she answered reluctantly, taking a step back as if recoiling from some imminent threat. Apparently, she wasn't used to being so boldly approached.

I was a bit cowed by her response, but since I hadn't spoken with any administrator since I arrived three days earlier, I seized the opportunity to ask a nagging question. "I'm a new substitute," I explained. "This is just my fourth day in the school. Can you tell me, are there any disciplinary guidelines for disruptive students that I should be aware of?"

She looked startled, as if she had suddenly encountered a rattlesnake. I hastily repeated, "I'm a new sub—new to this school and to the system, that is—and I'd like to know what your procedures are for dealing with discipline problems."

"What do you mean?" she retorted in a frosty voice that was anything but friendly.

I hadn't imagined that I was probing classified information. My take away from the all too brief orientation class was that all schools were required to have such a document on file.

"I mean, uh, what do I do if a child becomes so disruptive that he or she can't be contained in the classroom?"

She appeared momentarily stymied. Her face registered her annoyance. Apparently, no sub had ever asked this question before. "Well, I guess you could send him to the office," she said tersely, regaining her composure. "But I hope that won't happen," she added quickly, then turned abruptly on her heels and walked away before I could assault her with any more ridiculous questions. It wasn't until later that I discovered that she was the school's principal.

Although the principal had deemed me not worthy of notice, apparently somebody had been observing me and liked what they saw. Perhaps they just appreciated the fact that nobody from any of my classrooms had been sent to the office or that I arrived early every day. As they say, no good deed goes unpunished. On the last day of my first week, I was asked if I would return after the holidays and take a long-term assignment.

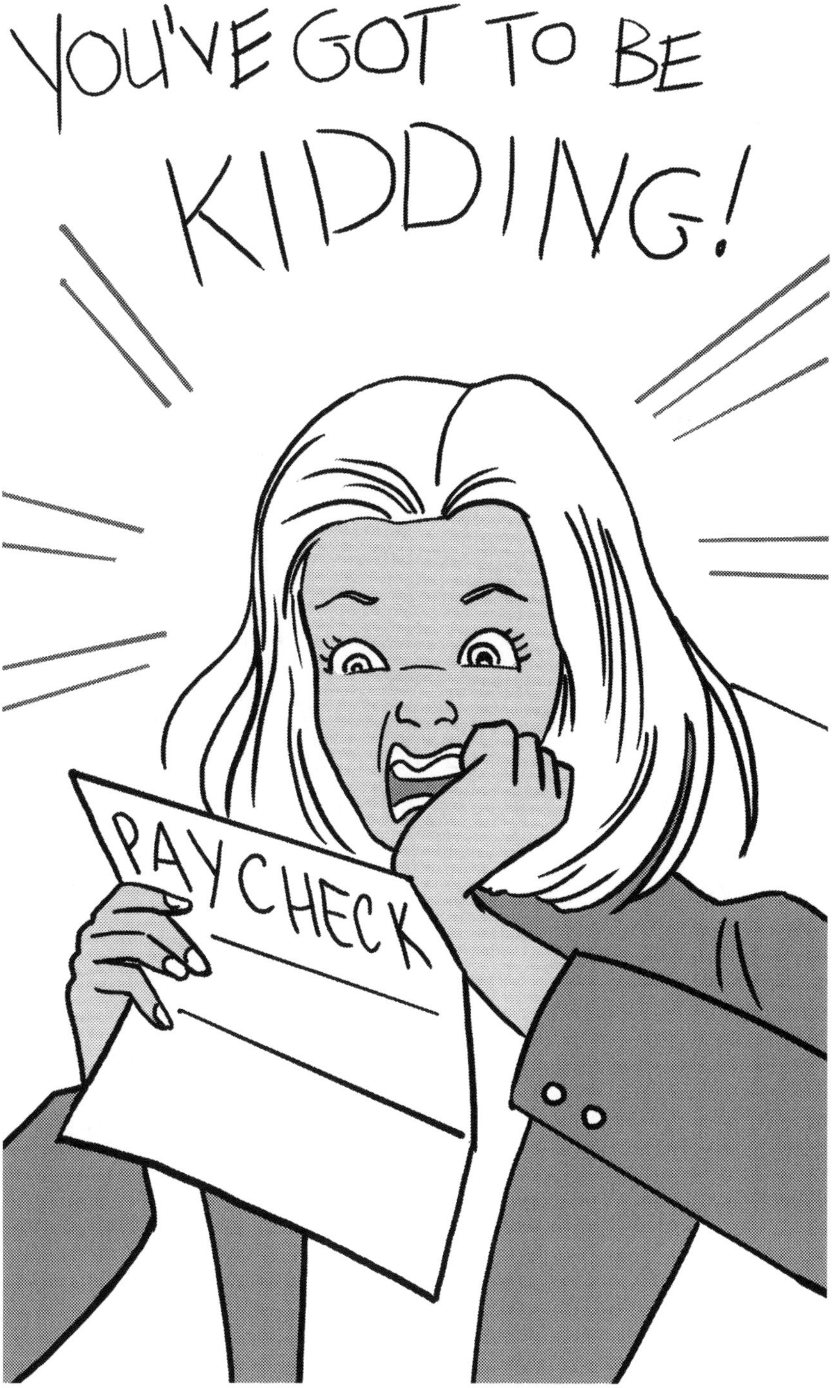
YOU'VE GOT TO BE KIDDING!
PAYCHECK

Rule 11: Read it and weep.

I was thoroughly pleased with myself. I had survived the multiple tests of my first full week and had been invited to return. Getting back into the classroom after an absence of more than two decades wasn't easy, I kid you not. But apparently I had made the grade.

I accepted the long-term offer without hesitation. It was a third grade position that was open because the teacher was going out for foot surgery and her recovery was expected to take at least three weeks, maybe longer. Perhaps I need look no further for a school I could call home because there would always be someone absent or on leave at Middle Town. I would spend the holidays in New York, get some good family stroking, and return fortified to meet the challenges of my brave new world.

The rate of pay for substitute teachers was $75 a day and increased to $90 with five or more consecutive days of subbing. I mentally calculated my earnings for the week and thought that my compensation for my first week of hard labor, after taxes, would be somewhere in the neighborhood of $400. Though it was in another realm from my publishing heydays, I consoled myself with the thought that it would at least pay for part of my holiday trip home.

Fortunately, since I had characteristically overspent, the check was waiting for me when I returned. Now, I've never liked those little self-sealed check holders. They're such a challenge to get into without destroying their contents, and my first thought is always that anything packaged like a two-dollar coupon can't be worth much.

To my surprise and utter dismay, I was right on target with that assessment. My check was written in the amount of two hundred two dollars and forty-seven cents! It was then that I discovered that, for payroll purposes, I had been classified as a paraprofessional substitute the two days I had worked in the kindergarten class. The daily rate for parapros was 45 dollars. It was the first time in my adult life that I, graduate school credentials notwithstanding, had essentially worked for minimum wage.

Rule 12: Put on the whole armor.

When I was told that the long-term assignment would be a third grade class, my first thought was this: How lucky can you get? Was I on a roll or what? My first teaching assignment at the beginning of my professional career had been in that grade. Experience was on my side. I knew how to relate to third graders. This was a good age. They weren't babies; I wouldn't have to wipe noses and tie shoelaces. They were young enough to still respect authority and old enough to know the difference between a teacher and a mother.

All of these preconceived notions went flying out of the window when I encountered Dak and Jude. There had never been a prototype for this duo. They were in a class all by themselves. Certainly, they weren't the only potential troublemakers in the class, but nobody could set it off like those two.

Dak, by himself, was manageable; never altogether good but containable. Jude, however, was from another realm. With him, there was no leverage. I later discovered that he was born to a heroin-addicted mother whose level of rehabilitation was unclear. Unknowingly, I made the mistake of threatening to send for his mother. That was apparently such a hoot that he literally laughed out loud. "Go ahead," he said smirking, and then muttered under his breath, "If you can find her."

Jude, a tall lanky nine-year-old, towered over the other children. He was handsome in a tough guy kind of way, like he had just stepped out of an old AMC spaghetti western. It was as if at any minute he would put his hands on his hips, look me dead straight in the eye and ask, "Whatcha lookin at pardna?" His good looks were marred, however, by a persistent scowl that was an integral part of his persona.

His comment about his mother hit me like a lightning bolt. I began to connect the dots. How utterly presumptuous of me to think that I could come into this class commanding this troubled child to stay in his seat and be a good little boy. His message was abundantly clear; nobody in his world was remotely interested in his performance or his progress, least of all, his mother.

I'm not ready for this, I thought. Too much has changed since I taught school. Nothing in my brief introduction to general school procedures had prepared me to deal with the lost boys and girls for whom nobody cares and who, in turn, care little or nothing about anything, including themselves. Jude, I soon discovered, was a clinical case; he needed clinical help. Fortunately for both of us, he was only in the classroom for two hours or so on any given day.

Dak could be contained; Jude could not. He was fearless and, unfortunately for me, he was also Dak's role model. When they combined their penchant for mischief, the two of them could take the class and me on one rocky roller coaster ride.

It would begin something like this: Jude would yell across to Dak, seated at the far opposite corner of the classroom. "Hey jelly belly."

Dak's reply: "Oogar oogar, sugar boogar."

Jude: "Tiddie widdie, booba looba."

Dak: Jigga bigga, booga boom."

And so it went as I racked my brain for the intervention of the day. Since Jude couldn't be threatened (What could a substitute teacher do to him that the world hadn't already done?) I usually tried to pick Dak off first. My only defense with Jude was distraction. The daily challenge was to entice him to focus on some other activity so the lesson could go forward. He was always in the room during the math period even though he wasn't capable of participating. He would leave in the morning for his special class as we began language arts, but return for lunch, recess and the rest of the afternoon.

I've never understood why the school would schedule something so mentally challenging and essential to the children's overall progress as math at the end of the day when their intellectual energy tanks were virtually running on fumes. It made no sense to me that a subject that could make or break them--considering the recent introduction of statewide mandated testing which would determine whether or not they passed on to the next grade--would be the last item on the school's daily academic agenda.

The schedule couldn't be altered. Students rotated to different classrooms for this period according to their performance levels, so juggling was not an option.

Thus, every day at 1:45 the fun began. Both Jude and Dak were in the room buzzing with unspent energy left over from recess and wired for action. Then, in marched another group of eight or nine fresh faces from other third grade classes, armed with math books and pencils, and ready for a different kind of action. The collision course was set, while each day at this time I offered up a silent prayer.

Sometimes Jude could be distracted with computer games or a trip to the library. The children all knew he was "different," so they never questioned his special privileges. Luckily, I discovered that he was fascinated with space travel and began bringing in every picture book on the subject I could lay my hands on. Often, I would talk to him about his books and supply him with an assortment of crayons and markers to create his own drawings. Some days it worked better than others.

Additionally, I allowed Jude free access to the various puzzles and construction toys in the interest center. His attention span was predictably short and when he tired of whatever he was doing, he'd rouse Dak and his other sycophants to keep him company.

My mornings (sans Jude) were going quite well, considering the fact that I never went to bed before one or two in the morning. On a typical school night, I'd be up grading papers and hatching out new, innovative lesson plan ideas into the wee hours. Afternoons were understandably the worst. Depending on Jude's moods and Dak's energy level, either or both of them could easily spin out of control.

I don't mean to suggest that these two were my only discipline problems. Far from it. But they were math lesson saboteurs One and Two. Other potential troublemakers included the pair I dubbed the Siamese twins, Brad and Rock, who were a Jude and Dak type buddy team, but not quite as bold or belligerent. Then there were the Jumping Jacks—Angel, Krystal, Jenny and Jared. These weren't bad or mean-spirited kids; they just had never learned to sit still for more than ten minutes without bolting out of their seats for one thing or another. Dominique was the sullen one who was forever kicking her classmates under her desk and the first to cry foul when they kicked back. Finally, there were the folk heroes, Liza and Chantay, who much to their classmates' amusement would blurt out loud any foul thoughts that popped into their heads.

The task of containing this hodge-podge of characters was tough enough, but as long as I could capture their attention and excite their interests, it was doable. During language arts sessions, we not only read the stories, we pantomimed the characters. Students were then encouraged to identify similar folk in their own families, communities or imagination and write stories about them. Often, they would get so involved in our numbers games during math lessons that some would ask to take their workbooks home on Fridays to complete a lesson, even though homework was not assigned on weekends. Everybody was learning something it seemed, except Jude who couldn't be taught, at least not by me.

After an initial couple days of frustration with the Dak and Jude problem, one of the teachers down the hall gave me a great suggestion for salvaging the math lesson when necessary. "Separate them," was her simple and profound suggestion for minimizing the disruptions. "When they threaten to spin out of control, move one of their desks out into the hallway," she suggested.

"Can you do that?" I asked. It was an option I had never even considered.

"Sure," she answered nonchalantly. "I do it all the time."

Which one to move was an easy decision. Dak, of course. He was, in fact, the only choice. Jude would refuse to go, and I would have painted myself into an impossible corner trying to make him do so. Besides, even if he agreed to move, there was no guarantee I would find him still there when the period ended. So Dak would be packed up—desk, chair, books and baggage—and moved just outside the door whenever the situation dictated desperate measures.

And, guess what? It worked! Dak even completed his math assignments, while Jude slouched sullenly in his chair and sometimes fell asleep. Obviously, clowning around without his cohort wasn't as much fun. And the class could be stimulated to tackle fractions, decimals and algebraic equations without interference. Little did I know I was breaking one of the cardinal rules in the book. Again, where was the book?

The practice of picking off the easier mark for the good of the group is one that I employed on several occasions. When I found myself losing control of the whole class, it sometimes worked to settle them down one at a time.

The positive approach was the first weapon in my arsenal. I rolled out the time-honored "time out" strategy that I had used back in the day. It had worked then, so it was worth a try. "Put your heads down on your desks," I commanded, "and only those students who demonstrate to me that they're interested in learning more about fractions today can participate. The rest of you don't have to participate if you don't want to, but you can't disturb the children who do want to learn."

Then, when the room was quiet, I'd begin polling them one-by-one. "Louise, do you want to learn something new today?" She was the best student in the class. Her response was predictably positive. "Okay, you may take out your workbook and open it to page 79." Same question to Allyson, Veronica, Latisha, Jonah, Steve, Jamillah and so on. Suddenly, learning became a privilege. Soon enough, the disrupters would be frantically trying to catch my eye, silently pleading their case for inclusion. They were children after all and could still be persuaded, by and large, to do the right thing.

But the bag of tricks had to be varied. Nothing works all the time. So, when the carrot failed to yield the desired results, I resorted to the stick. As I stated earlier, most of the problems popped up during the math hour. That is also, I think, understandably, when my coping mechanisms were most depleted. On this particular day, I was tasked with administering a required math test. The children were restless; even the weather wasn't cooperating.

It had rained all day, right through recess. Consequently, outdoor recess had been cancelled, and getting the kids settled after indoor recess was a lengthier process. Outdoor recess had a distinct beginning and ending; with indoor, they never wanted to give up the games and go back to work. But settle down they must, because a math test had to be executed.

The regular curriculum schedule was one to which I religiously adhered. Nevertheless, I opted out of the statewide testing for the third graders when the tests had to be given individually—and on the computer! How in the world did they expect a substitute, who could barely turn her back to write on the board, to administer tests that required the teacher to go one-on-one and sit for forty or more minutes a pop in a room where vigilant patrolling was required for all activities throughout the day? If the tests were that essential and achievement levels to be accurately measured, why wasn't some assistance available to the substitute for that phase of the assignment? I had simply balked and without apology ignored that part of the lesson plan. I may be compulsive, but delusional I am not.

However, I did test them regularly as a group as indicated in their language arts and math schedules. There was always a preparation ritual, particularly for math. Dak would be sent to his isolation booth just outside the door and Jude was given a generous supply of space books, drawing materials and free access to a computer. The rest of the class faced the threat of a failing grade if they had to be excluded from test-taking for disruptive behavior. Usually it worked.

Rule 13: Don't talk to strangers.

Look for them by land and they come by sea. The problem on this particular day was Krystal, one of the Jumping Jacks. Normally, she was not one who gave me any prolonged grief. Sometimes I thought she needed to be chained to her seat but, other than that, she was generally a good kid. And a good student. Little did I suspect that a confrontation with Krystal would have such serious repercussions.

I liked Krystal. There was nothing mean-spirited about her. She always had a warm greeting for me in the morning and generally sought my approval for her work. Like most of her classmates, she was normally on her best behavior during the first half of the day. But she could be distracted in an instant. On any given day, quick as a flash, this skinny, agile child would bounce out of her seat and flit across the room to engage in lively conversation with a friend before I could say, "Sit down!" My private name for her was Chatty Cathy, and like the talkative doll of old, she periodically needed to be unplugged.

Well, this just wasn't my day. Krystal, along with the rest of the class was fidgety. Blame it on the weather. Getting the Jumping Jacks to sit still after indoor recess had taken longer than usual, cutting seriously into the time allocated for the required weekly math test. As it happened, Krystal was the sole holdout when the rest of the class was finally ready to get down to business.

Once order was established and the testing was underway, Krystal was the only one who just wouldn't stop talking. Her nearest neighbor, Louise, who was undoubtedly the most serious and accomplished student in the class, was trying to distance herself from the miscreant. Louise kept aiming eye appeals in my direction in a desperate plea for help. I suspect Krystal was unprepared and pressing Louise for answers but, whatever her motivation, I understood that Louise just wanted to be left alone to complete her test.

"Krystal!" I admonished her three or more times. "Stop talking!" In the classroom, defiance is contagious. It wouldn't be long before others, observing my inability to contain Krystal, decided to follow suit.

Something had to be done before Krystal's defiance escalated into a bigger control situation. She and her classmates needed to understand that no one had the right to disrupt the testing environment. To my surprise, Krystal was clearly calling my bluff and continued to audibly lean into Louise's ear. Finally, in an act of desperation, I snatched up her paper and ordered her to put her head down on her desk. Then I scrawled a big "0" across the top of the page in bright red ink and drew a line at the bottom of the page with this demand: "Signature of Parent."

There it was for all the class to see. I had delivered on the threat; the statement had to be made. Disruptive students would be dealt with in a decisive manner during test periods and there would be no appeal. The Louises in the class have a right to demonstrate their progress without running interference. A dejected Krystal ducked her head onto her desk sobbing audibly, and the test proceeded without further interruption.

The consequences of this little encounter were manifested sooner than I ever could have imagined. The incident occurred on Tuesday; on Wednesday, I got an early morning surprise.

I felt drained the next day and had arrived a bit later than usual, having been up well past midnight writing lesson plans and grading test papers. This business demanded instant gratifications. Students needed to see the results of yesterday's exam and other assignments as soon as possible to evaluate the success or failure upon which to build their goals before the next round of lessons.

The drive to work was just under an hour. I could have worked closer to home, but traveling to this school meant going against the traffic, which afforded me some extra time for sifting and sorting the elements of my pending school day.

I was still putting the morning's story-starter on the board when the students began arriving. Suddenly, I looked up to see two adults with a young baby standing behind me. The woman, who at first glance came across as matronly and fortyish, perhaps due to the tension registered on her face, was, upon closer scrutiny, rather pretty in a girl-next-door sort of way. Her somewhat disheveled hair and mismatched attire suggested that she had dressed hurriedly. The man, tall, gaunt and menacing, didn't allow me much time to size him up. Before I could greet them and ask for their visitors' pass, he lashed out at me, waving Krystal's math test of the previous afternoon in my face and snarling.

"Are you Miss Crawley's substitute?" he asked in a highly confrontational, disrespectful voice.

"I'm Miss Miles," I said, attempting to conceal my astonishment. "How may I help you?"

"You can start by telling me the meaning of this," he said, his voice seething with anger.

"And who are you, may I ask?" I was regaining my composure.

"I'm Krystal's stepfather and this is her mother," he bellowed, quite red in the face and still waving the paper. "Now answer the question. What is the meaning of this?"

"Didn't Krystal tell you?" Aha, I thought, as I assessed his attitude. He's obviously trying to impress the mother that he's up to the job of step parenting.

"I'm asking *you*," he replied in a voice that was even more menacing.

"Can we step outside?" I said, ushering them through the door. We were beginning to attract an audience.

When we were outside the door and not as easily overheard by inquiring little ears, I continued. "As I'm sure Krystal explained, the class was taking a math test. Krystal had been asked repeatedly to stay in her seat and stop talking. When my several requests went unheeded, she left me no choice but to exclude her from the test."

"Nonsense," he retorted, dismissing my explanation. "Krystal said the other girl was talking to her."

I could see where this was going, so I asked Krystal, who was standing in the hallway with her parents, to go inside and start her work.

"Well, *I'm* telling you, Krystal was the one creating the disturbance," I resumed once Krystal was in the room. "The other student just happens to be one of the most diligent workers in the class, and she was attempting to take her test, which she is entitled to do without running interference."

"Well, that's not the way I heard it," he insisted, while the mother stood silently by, bouncing the baby and allowing him to do all the talking. I guessed she was being duly impressed with his assertiveness in his surrogate father role. "And anyway," he continued belligerently, "Aren't you just the substitute? You'll be gone in a few days and crap like this will still be on Krystal's record. Where do you get off anyway?" Apparently, he was enjoying his own show.

I wasn't. Holding my rising anger in check, I demanded, "What did you say to Krystal," I asked. "Did you say anything to her about her behavior?"

"What we say to our daughter is our business," he snapped. "I'm talking to you and I want some answers."

I made another attempt to explain the situation to him, but he was entirely intransigent. His language became increasingly more abusive. "You don't know what you're doing," he raged, "and I'm not going to let you mess over this child's grades because you don't know what the hell you're doing." With this last verbal assault, he took a step forward and got in my face just a little too close for comfort.

That's it, I said to myself. Maybe his wife was impressed, but I wasn't. And I wasn't taking any more abuse from him, especially in front of Krystal and the rest of the class, all of whom had now assembled and sat on the edge of their seats to witness the encounter through the open door. There was not even a cough or a sneeze breaking the heavy silence.

"If you'll excuse me, I have a class to teach," I said, abruptly ending the sideshow. "If you want to speak with me further, please make an appointment." With that, I turned on my heels, raised my head high and walked into the room, closing the door behind me.

Before day's end, I heard, for the first time, from the principal.

The summons came in the late afternoon over the intercom for all the class to hear: "Miss Miles, would you stop by Miss Green's office before you leave today." Silence gripped the room. The message had an ominous ring to it. Miss Green was the assistant principal whom I had never met either.

On my way out, I stopped by Miss Green's office. The AP sat rigidly at her desk wearing a serious but inscrutable face. I had the impression that this was not her normal demeanor. She had been gifted with a round, naturally pleasant face and seemed to be working hard at contorting it into a more authoritative facade. The conversation was short and to the point. "Oh, Miss Miles, Ms. Spencer (so the principal did have a name) would like to meet with you at 10 o'clock tomorrow morning in her office," she announced flatly.

"Oh," I replied. "Can you tell me what about?"

"She has some things she wants to discuss with you," said Green, returning to the papers she had been shuffling on her desk, signaling that there was nothing more to be said. I noted that the conference had been scheduled for my one free period in the day. Obviously, they had looked it up.

Rule 14: Know when to fold.

Of course, I lost sleep that night. Chronic insomniac that I am, it doesn't take much to keep me tossing and turning the whole night. I even flirted with the idea that there was no connection between the hostile encounter with Krystal's father and the meeting; that Ms. Spencer perhaps wanted to commend me for the job I was doing and invite me to sign on for a permanent position in the fall. The timing with the Krystal incident could be coincidental, I reasoned. But I didn't really believe it.

When I walked into the principal's office the following morning, she and Ms. Green were already seated, waiting for me. Their body language gave the plot away. This was not a meeting; it was an inquisition. They got right to the point. Green had been designated to go first. She opened a folder and shuffled several sheets of paper. I couldn't imagine how someone to whom I had never spoken could have compiled a dossier that deep. At the top of the heap, staring at me from across the table was Krystal's aborted test paper.

The assistant principal voiced her concern from the parent's vantage point before even asking me what had happened. Krystal, she would have me know, was a good student and not a known discipline problem. The parents had legitimate concerns. I should understand that tests are learning tools, an opportunity for students to demonstrate their progress and simultaneously alert teachers to their learning needs. They were not intended to be used as instruments for punishment.

Next, it was Spencer's turn. "Things have changed a lot since you were in the school system," she began. "You'll find that we do things differently now." Okay, okay. Playing the age card, huh? Translate that to mean you are something of a relic; outdated, obsolete, and you're damned lucky to have this job. Now shrink in your seat and take this reprimand.

On one thing Spencer and I could agree: Things really have changed. I contrasted the behavior or Krystal's stepfather to that of an irate parent I had summoned to come up to school to report her child's misbehavior in my old teaching days. That parent had been very hostile too, but for a different reason. "Why are you sending for me?" she had yelled. "Why can't you handle this problem? Don't you have any paddles in this school?"

Well paddles weren't the answer then and certainly not now. But at least that parent hadn't wanted to paddle me.

I was livid. I would have taken the beat down better if either of them had ever shown the slightest interest in what was happening in my classroom before this incident. Maybe if they had even asked to hear my side of the story, I could have taken the scolding in stride. Yes, I was only a substitute but I wasn't a child, and I was entitled to a certain amount of respect. Following a pregnant pause, I regrouped. Okay. If that's the way you want to play it, let's do it. They weren't prepared for my response.

I told them that I hadn't come to baby sit; that I had been hired to teach. Teaching, and especially testing, required a certain amount of order in the classroom. Just what methods did they recommend to contain a discipline problem such as Krystal had created? I asked. I reminded Spencer that I had requested the school's discipline procedures in the first week of my assignment and had yet to receive such. I also reminded her that the only suggestion she offered was to send the disruptive child to the office. Obviously, that was not a solution to be used with every infraction unless the substitute was prepared to surrender control of the classroom, I pointed out.

They were visibly stunned. I could read their thoughts. Didn't I realize how plentiful substitutes are in this economy and how expendable I was; that I ought to be groveling and pleading for a second chance? Obviously not. It was time to fire the big guns. Green leafed through her folder before unleashing her next missile.

"On several occasions, when walking past your classroom, I've seen Dak sitting in the hallway. Do you realize that is a school safety violation? We are responsible for the safety and wellbeing of our students every minute of the school day. At no time are they ever to be unsupervised."

I was momentarily stymied. It seemed I had been given some bad advice. But, "several times," she said. Why hadn't she called this to my attention the *first* time? Why now? I felt a rising sense of outrage. Is this how the system works? The administration allows us to break the rules, and then confronts us at their convenience. If the rule was intended to protect the children's safety, why was it only arbitrarily enforced? I speculated that as long as I kept the little monsters contained and didn't traffic in and out of the office with the disruptives it wasn't a problem. That is, as long as they didn't get any complaints from parents.

Spencer picked up the baton. Apparently, they were well rehearsed in their tag team routine. "We're told you write children's names on the board. What is that about?"

I felt beads of perspiration accumulating on my upper lip. They had succeeded in putting *me* on the defensive. I heard myself stammering.

"Well, uh," I cleared my throat, "it's nothing very serious. It just, uh, means that they could miss recess or some other activity if they don't settle down and get to work. But they always have the opportunity to demonstrate good behavior and get their names removed."

"That's a total violation of school rules," Spencer stated emphatically, emboldened by my obvious discomfort.

School rules? Again, what rules? Now she was going to tell me the rules!

"You should understand that the specials (music, art, physical education) are an essential part of the core curriculum. Depriving students of these learning opportunities is never an acceptable disciplinary option."

She had me. What could I say? Try the truth.

"Well, it's something I've never had to do. It works because I've never actually had to follow through and keep any child from any of those classes." What I didn't say was that depriving students of their specials was an alternative no teacher would welcome, because keeping one kid behind for an individual lesson would mean more work for the teacher and a lost period for planning and organizing. I was always happy to let them earn release from the threatened disciplinary action.

"Well, you should never threaten anything you're not prepared to follow through on," Spencer sniffed.

I felt hot beads of moisture stinging the corners of my eyes. Please God, I prayed, hold back the tears. I was fuming now. I had walked into a bad situation. This class, in the collective opinion of the other third grade teachers and other school personnel, was about the worst behaved in the building. I was doing the job of a teacher and, according to my colleagues in the third grade cluster, a far better job than their regular teacher for a fraction the pay. This was a fact that everybody else in the school seemed to recognize and appreciate except my accusers. Yet, they could tell me about names on the board. Offering me no support was one thing, but calling me on the carpet because of one irate parent was quite another. It was my turn to confront them.

"Are you telling me you don't know that this is a difficult class?"

"What do you mean?" Spencer asked dumbly, apparently caught off guard by the counterattack.

"It's a fact that everybody else in your school seems to be aware of," I said, not backing down. "The students have poor work habits and the class has a disproportionate number of discipline problems. Establishing some order, including basic things like cleaning up the room, and general procedures and routines (I hoped I wasn't babbling) to create an environment where learning can take place has been a monumental challenge."

She was not deterred. Principals are apparently not accustomed to such "insubordination." This one, especially, would not take it well, having been a drill sergeant in the military before pursuing a career in education. It was time to fire her biggest bullet.

"Well, if you feel that way about it, would you want to continue?" she asked.

Funny you should ask, I thought. "As a matter of fact, I don't," I said calmly. I could feel a weight being lifted even as I made my decision.

They were visibly shocked. I could tell by the furtive eye exchanges that this was an unintended outcome. They had only meant to intimidate and browbeat me so they could go back to Krystal's parents and report that I had been duly reprimanded. My resignation was not in the game plan.

Now it was Green's turn to stammer. "Well, uh, uh, you will finish out the week, won't you?"

I deliberated for a few moments. "What's today?" I asked rhetorically. "Thursday? Yes, I could do that. I'll come in tomorrow."

The conference was over. There was nothing more to say so I excused myself.

Rule 15: Cut the last class

Later, I would have one big regret: Why hadn't I taken them to task for not admonishing the parents who had stormed into my classroom without a pass? Speaking of violations, surely this was one with potentially far greater consequences than names on the board or a missed special. Why had they even listened to them if they had invaded my classroom illegally? What about security in this age of school shootings and attacks on teachers?

Somehow, I managed to get through the rest of the day. When I returned, a hushed silence permeated the classroom. Maybe the kids were reading my face and could see that I was in no mood for nonsense.

When I shared the outcome of my conference with the teachers in the cluster after dismissal, they were outraged.

"I'm sick of this," said one. "That's why we can't get good teachers."

"Go to the district office," advised another. "You never know what they're going to put in your record."

"Write to the superintendent," another suggested. "They need to know what goes on in these schools."

"The children are the losers," said another sadly. "Heaven only knows who they're going to get to replace you."

I thanked them warmly for their kind condolences. I appreciated their concern but knew I wouldn't be following up on any of their suggestions. I hadn't come there for a fight. Between my failed business and unfaithful husbands, I'd had enough battles for one lifetime.

In truth, I felt as though a big load had been lifted, and I didn't give a hoot *what* they put in my folder. I knew that I had no intention of ever returning to that school district or any other for that matter. As far as I was concerned, my brief career as a substitute teacher was over. Unfortunately, my ordeal wasn't.

Marla, my friend across the hall couldn't understand why I was bothering to come in the next day. If she had been treated so shabbily, she would have walked out then and there, she said. But as corny as it sounds, it was about the children. They were about to have to adjust to yet another change. There were a few things I wanted to wrap up and, for the sake of continuity, leave some notes for my successor. Besides, there was only one day left in the week.

Marla was right and I was wrong. Just how wrong, I would soon discover.

The next morning, the atmosphere in the classroom was charged. You could feel it; you could hear it. Mornings were usually quiet times. By now, my third graders were accustomed to finding their assignments on the board when they arrived, sharpening pencils before going to their seats, and settling into their morning work without much fanfare. But this morning things were different. The entire class was unsettled. They were flitting about the room from one corner to the next engaged in animated chatter. It was rare that I had to raise my voice any more during the first period. But on this fateful Friday, it was impossible to calm them down. Finally, little Ken sought me out and confided, "Miss Miles, Krystal's spreading a rumor that you got fired."

"Yes," others chimed in. "Is that true, Miss Miles?"

It hit me like a bolt of lightning. I was appalled. This was a level of un-professionalism I could never have fathomed. But there was no other way of explaining it. Apparently, Spencer or Green had gotten on the phone yesterday to square things with Krystal's parents, not even bothering to wait until I had completed the assignment. Marla had been so right; I should not have come back. Basically, I'm not a quitter, but having folded my hand, I should have run for the nearest exit.

The day promised to be punishing. Dak was the first to seize the moment. His message to the class, both in words and deeds was this: You don't have to worry about Miss Miles anymore. She won't be here after today. Krystal's father got her fired, so we can do what we damn well please. And that's exactly what he proceeded to do. He had declared war; he would have to suffer the consequences.

Dak, I reasoned, was no longer my problem. The administrators had empowered this little rascal to go berserk on me, so they could have the pleasure of dealing with him. I sat down and fired off this note:

Dear Ms. Spencer,

The rumor is rampant in the classroom that Krystal is telling her classmates, "Miss Miles got fired and isn't coming back."

The point has to be made that today is business as usual and not a holiday. I can't understand how anyone, least of all an administrator, would give a parent or student that kind of ammunition when I'm expected to teach a class today. And, obviously, you know it isn't true.

Please be reminded that I was not fired! I asked to be released!

When I finished my note, I commanded the startled boy to pack up his belongings and marched him off to the office. It was the first time I had seen him cry.

Spencer was not there. None of the clerks took issue with me. Now, it was I who was firing off the questions: "Where is Ms. Spencer?" "When is she coming back?" "Having created this chaos today, how does she expect me to control this class?" Then, no longer cognizant of *my place* I demanded, "Tell her I would like to speak with her as soon as she returns."

I never got that opportunity. I wasn't surprised since I already knew how skilled she was at dodging encounters. However, she did write this one-line reply, which was handed to me at the end of the day:

No one from this office has stated to anyone that you have been fired!
So, guess what? She was also a liar.

The third grade teachers wrote much more. At lunchtime, they hastily got together and bought me a bouquet of flowers. It was a simple arrangement of the mixed garden variety sold in supermarkets, but it was then and will always be one of the most cherished gifts I have ever received because of the thoughts that came with it. I quote verbatim from the card that accompanied the flowers. Only the names have been changed.

"We all know what a great teacher you are and how much you have given to these children. Thank you."
Kathy
"You were music for this class."
Marla
"God always places people in our paths for various reasons. I thank God for you and all your efforts and concerns you have illustrated for our children. May the Lord keep you and grant all of your desires, according to his will."
Donna
"I want you to know that you and your efforts have not gone unnoticed nor unappreciated. You have been wonderful!"
Ellie
"You were fabulous for that class."
Allison
"We will miss you. Don't let what happened here destroy your joy. You are a wonderful and beautiful person"
Valerie
"Laura and the class were fortunate to have you! We all will miss you."
Gloria

I was tremendously moved. With a scant half hour lunch break, how had they found the time to shop for flowers, to say nothing of circulating a card with such thoughtful farewells? They had only known me three weeks. Apparently, I had done something right.

As I packed to leave, the tears finally fell. It wasn't about my situation; I could get another job, especially if I was willing to settle for my current rate of pay. They were tears of gratitude for those wonderful people who had taken stock of what I was endeavoring to do with this class and had interrupted their day to express such appreciation. It was also about the parent, mother of one of the other Jumping Jacks, who had stopped by to express her dismay at the turn of events.

"My daughter likes you so much," she said, "and she's really excited about school again. Do you really have to leave? Would it help if some of us, some parents I mean, talked to Miss Spencer?"

And yes, I was sad for *them*, the mélange of faces—curious, indifferent, some even hostile—that would greet my replacement on Monday. And, okay, I'll admit it; it was about Krystal too. What about Krystal? What are we saying to the child when the message translates that you can win disciplinary conflicts when you come to school unprepared by summoning your parents to get the teacher "fired"? Krystal would have been given a make-up test. That was always in the game plan, but the dispute was never really about her grade.

The real message, in my case anyway, was that a substitute is a nobody, without tenure or support, who can be summarily dismissed with or without cause. Do we really want to put that kind of power into the hands of students or parents? Teachers get an average of twelve to fifteen sick or personal leave days each school year. And don't forget maternity and other long-term absences. Most teachers I know, understandably, max out on their leave time in any given school year. Isn't it in the best interest of the schools and the students to support real learning activities during these absences, especially with so much emphasis on test results?

I left this one school with more respect for the classroom teacher than I had ever known. I have gained a whole new appreciation for the job they do. Nothing about it is easy; every day is a challenge.

I'm reminded of the joke one of my colleague's husband would make about our profession in my early days of teaching. "My wife doesn't work," he would say sarcastically. "She teaches school." Ha! Wonder what he would say if he could spend a few hours in today's classroom. Guess he'd have to revise his definition of work.

Several of the teachers shared tales of their own ordeals at Middle Town. Most memorable was Marla's story.

Marla was my role model, one of the most gifted and dedicated teachers I've ever known. Her classroom was directly across the hall from mine so I had ample opportunities to observe her in action. She was my go-to person for my many classroom dilemmas. I had a habit of popping in and out of her room with my urgent distress calls. Each time I crossed her threshold I witnessed some exciting, stimulating lesson in progress. You can't fake those scenes—Marla with an overhead projector making math an adventure; children sitting around her in a semicircle fully engaged in a language arts lesson; the quiet buzz of children working together productively in small groups on some creative project as she moved lithely from one group to the next, spurring them on to greater achievement. In my estimation, she deserved a very tall pedestal. She would easily have been my nominee for Teacher of the Year in any competition.

But, instead of getting her much-deserved accolades, she had been written up by the district supervisor. Her problem? She loved what she was doing too much. Her only desire was to remain in the classroom just being a good teacher. It seems that Spencer had something else in mind for her. When organizing her staff at the new school, I'm told she had attempted to pull Marla out of the classroom to become her assistant principal, although Marla had expressed no such interest. Yes, she had a Ph.D. from a good eastern university and was fully qualified to run the whole school and perhaps the district, too. But all she really wanted to do was teach.

Marla wasn't seeking recognition or commendations for her performance and, obviously, she wasn't courting promotion. Her reward was the enjoyment she derived from working with children, molding them into good students eager to learn and helping them realize their full academic potential.

According to Marla, and as several of her co-workers attested, Spencer took exception to her refusal and began giving her a hard time. With her regimented military background, she evidently was not used to taking no for an answer. Or maybe she thought that by piling on extra duties and judging her classroom performance with extreme prejudice, Marla would eventually cave and join the administration team. When Marla complained to the district supervisor about the unfair treatment, she was written up for insubordination, an assessment that still remains in her file.

Chapter Three

———∿∿———

Survival of the Fittest

Obviously, after a mere three weeks on the job and given my colossal demise, I'm hardly an authority on substitute teaching. While I'm reluctant to offer career counseling to new or prospective subs, my parting thought is this: Consider your options. Substitute teaching is not an easy job by any stretch of the imagination. The challenges are great and the rewards are few. If you have the stamina and the right attitude, I suppose it can work. I obviously didn't have enough of either.

Since then, I've moved on to other things, and the school system, including Wilton County, seems to be surviving without me. I must confess, however, that I did get a rather perverse satisfaction every day at around 6 p.m. when my phone would ring with a call from the district's automated system to request a substitute. I didn't remove my name from the list for several months because I did so much enjoy pressing the "No" button. No, I won't accept an assignment for tomorrow. No, I don't want any more calls this evening. And although you didn't ask, NO, I'm never going back there again.

It is a given that schools will always need substitutes and, whether they realize it or not, so do parents and administrators. It is probably also true that there will always be abuses on all sides of the spectrum. My experience wasn't a good one, but I know people who substitute regularly and actually enjoy their work.

My friend Amy is a case in point. She subs three or more times a week in several schools near her home. She thinks it's a great post-retirement job because it doesn't bind her to a regular schedule and she can accept or refuse assignments on any given day. She's able to supplement her income and still enjoy the freedom and flexibility of traveling, shopping or lunching with friends whenever she chooses.

Amy says the secret of her success is never accepting a long-term assignment. "I don't mind babysitting," she explains, "and a day or two in any one classroom is enough for me." She follows a lesson plan if one is available, but doesn't sweat it if there isn't.

"What do you do with them in that case," I asked.

"Whatever they want to do," she said candidly. "It's not my job to make lesson plans. They don't pay me enough for that."

"But don't the children get pretty unruly if you don't provide them some structure," I prodded.

"As long as they don't kill each other, I don't worry about it," she said cavalierly.

"Anyway, I'm only there for a day or so, and whatever I do isn't going to make that much difference. I take a newspaper or magazine or one of my tech toys to keep me occupied. The only thing I'm missing is ear plugs. And I keep my mind focused on that nice glass of wine I'm going to enjoy as soon as I go home."

I contrasted Amy's approach to subbing with mine. She has mapped out a survival strategy and comes away unscathed at the end of the day. I was busy trying to be "wonder woman" and got "fired" retroactively for my efforts. Who was right and who was wrong? Perhaps neither or both of us. The truth may lie somewhere in between, but I couldn't stick around to find out.

In recent conversations with friends still in the school system, I gather that not a lot has changed since my brief sojourn. Or, as the familiar adage suggests, "The more things change, the more they remain the same." If anything, given today's budget battles and war on teachers, things may even have gotten worse.

Probably the only conclusion you can draw from what you've just read is that everyone's experience is different. Amy and I were poles apart in our approaches to the job. She survived and I didn't. So, if you're still inclined to give it a try, I say go for it and good luck.

JOIN THE CONVERSATION.
TeachersTalkNow.com

Printed in the United States
By Bookmasters